LIFE. DEATH. LOVE & CONNECTION

KIM PETERSEN
WITH XAVIER EASTENBRICK

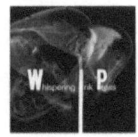

Life. Death. Love & Connection

CONTENTS

Introduction ix

1. I Am A Bird — 1
2. The Art of Kissing — 6
3. Love Doesn't Always Mean Monogamy — 11
4. Tribes — 20
5. Getting Real — 26
6. The Unreal — 31
7. Greenhorn — 36
8. Give and Take — 42
9. Living from the Heart — 48
10. Rock, Stars & Signs — 54
11. Karmic Dad — 61
12. Who Needs People? You do. — 68
13. Rooms for the Memory – What's it Really About Anyway? — 76
14. The Girl Can Shine — 82
15. Scandalous: A Fleeting Love Song — 89
16. Dirty Dancing — 98
17. It's a Sex Type Thing — 103
18. Love on a Train — 109
19. Sexual Transmutation and Alchemy — 115
20. Who Wants A Virgin Anyway? — 121
21. Superheroes — 127
22. Parenting in the Fast Lane — 132
23. Abuse Me, Abuse Me Not — 137
24. Some Apologies Are Endless — 144
25. Friendship is Like Treasure — 148

26. Change – What Light's You Up on the Inside?	154
27. Heartbeat – A Woman's Right	165
28. Go ahead, be offended. You have that right	171
29. Relationships and the Power of Standing Your Ground	181
30. The Whisper	188
31. Where's the Excitement At?	195

SOUL SIGNATURES

1. The Twin Flame Soul Connection Series by Xavier Eastenbrick	205
2. Runner & Chasers	216
3. The Awakening	228
Thank You	249
About the Authors	251

Whispering Ink: Life. Death. Love & Connection.
© copyright 2020 Whispering Ink Press

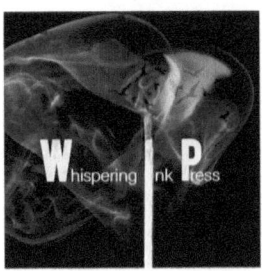

All rights reserved under the International and Pan-American Copyright Conventions. No part of this book may be reproduced or transmitted in any form or by any means, electronic or mechanical, including photocopying, recording, or by any information storage and retrieval system, without permission in writing from the publisher. This is a work of fiction. Names, places, characters and incidents are either the product of the author's imagination or are used fictitiously, and any resemblance to any actual persons, living or dead, organizations, events or locales is entirely coincidental. Warning: the unauthorized reproduction or distribution of this copyrighted work is illegal. Criminal copyright infringement, including infringement without monetary gain, is investigated by the FBI and is punishable by up to 5 years in prison and a fine of $250,000. This is a Whispering Ink Press book brought to you by Whispering Ink Press.

eBook IBSN: 978-0-6485491-4-7

Paperback IBSN: 978-0-6485491-3-0

Edited by Paul Vander Loos

Cover Design by Paradox Book Covers & Formatting

INTRODUCTION

In 2016, I created a blog because I had read someplace that an author should have a blog as part of their online presence. I was new on the publishing scene, having written and published one novel with limited knowledge and without much of a solid plan.

Alas, I did what I thought I should be doing – I created a website, organized paid promotion and began networking with other authors. Then, the blog came along.

The problem was, although I had these great plans to use this interactive platform to write about topics that matter, and hopefully relate to other people, I didn't have the courage to get vulnerable enough to express myself in that way.

Until now.

2019 has been a transformational year for me. It was a year that forced me to face my inner-darkness and fears, as well as the light and love within; a year dedicated to soul-growth, laying new foundations and stretching my perspective. A year spent forming and cultivating a relationship with my authentic self on a deeper level.

Writing blog posts has been a big part of this journey.

There are times in our lives when we get to choose which path to take – the easy way is, well, easy. It requires playing it safe, resisting change and staying put. It requires little effort and risk on our part.

There is nothing wrong with playing it safe. But keeping the walls up denies us opportunities to bond with one another. It rejects new ideas, pushes against our natural state to reach for more and broaden our perspectives.

Living this way doesn't feed the soul nor catapult us into becoming the best version of ourselves. This way is to remain as you are - to exist in a way that denies your soul what it seeks above all else; expansion. Love. This way is the ordinary way.

Opportunity for soul growth can arrive through various mediums. Sometimes, and quite usually, exponential growth is followed when we experience a crisis of some nature. Other times, it is when we encounter those who spark something dormant within that causes a significant shift to take place at a deeper level.

How can you explain to someone who doesn't understand what happens when we encounter a significant other? How can you communicate the real magic of deep connection and the creativity born from the fusion to someone who hasn't experienced it?

It is near impossible, but I'll try.

Real connection will rattle your senses to ignite change. It will feel as if a key turned within your soul to open a door you never knew existed. Once you cross the threshold, there is no way to "unknow" all that is revealed – which is everything beautiful and dark within.

Most of all, it is through these sacred people that touch our lives that we find the courage to free ourselves of limited thinking; the courage to be bold with our creativity and find the spirit to become who we are meant to become.

I found the courage to explore and question myself, and the world. As well as the courage to write in new ways and dare to envision an alternative future.

It is when we are willing to die to our former selves to embrace new ways of thinking and being that we truly grasp the meaning of existence. This isn't some New Age quack notion - life is about getting vulnerable, living big and loving furiously. It is about taking risks, connecting to others and sharing our experiences in order to help each other grow. It's being brave enough to take the messy path because you sense it's worth deep in your bones.

This year, I chose to shed a part of myself in order to emerge into myself.

Does that make sense?

INTRODUCTION

A large part of this process is still being played out through the words I create and share with whoever takes the time to listen.

Most of us are aware that storytelling has been used to articulate the experiences and tribulations of our earliest ancestors to guide, teach and inform. Through the ages, story has existed to provide cautionary warnings to their predecessors, but it also through storytelling that we have searched for the sacred dimension of life.

Blogs are an exceptional platform for the continuation of this kind of storytelling. Posting our words enable us to share personal experiences - to teach, connect with and help one another. They provide a way that allows us to get real and gritty; to explore life and everything encompassing the human experience.

Through sharing words and telling my life experiences on my blog, *Whispering Ink*, I have worked through parts of my life to bring a collection of posts designed to connect with people; and hopefully a small part of that body of work found the person in most need of reading the words.

If I achieved that, then I am forever grateful.

This year has been a year of revolution. In facing my own insecurities and fears, I have been able to embrace a new version of myself – a woman who is slowly learning to believe in herself. A woman who has been reminded of higher-love and what it means to accept the things she

INTRODUCTION

cannot change - who took a deep breath and published some of the deepest parts of herself.

As the end of the year looms on the horizon, I look back on the struggles 2019 brought with a sense of gratitude. I took risks and stepped out of my comfort zone more times than I care to recount. I laughed and cried; I weaved through confusion and told the people that matter how I feel. I wrote words that reflected a journey lived with heart and shared those stories with the world.

I regret nothing.

In the end, it is our willingness to be authentic that counts. It is through connection and reflection that ignite inner-growth. But it is through the creation of words and sharing our experiences that fosters the power of true expansion.

The following is an accumulation of the words and stories reflecting my journey throughout 2019 - including some very special contributions from my friend, Xavier Eastenbrick, who was kind enough to share his insight along the way. These words may not matter to everyone, but they matter to me and it is my hope that you will find something of value within this book.

With love,
Kim

I AM A BIRD

When my mother was pregnant with me, my parents moved to a tidy brick, semi-detached home nestled in a quiet street in the southern suburbs of Sydney. There was huge tree on the street outside our home, and the front yard had two small sections of lawn. The gardens were minimal but well maintained thanks to my father, and the backyard was a huge concrete oasis – which was fabulous when your six years old and you ride a bike like the wind. Not so great when you stack it, though. There were no push-bike helmets in the 80's, but I survived.

Rockdale.

Honestly, and I've never admitted this to another soul – I was never proud to be born and raised in that suburb. It's not that I'm ashamed, I guess the town has served a purpose in shaping my life. It's through these contrasts that we learn what we don't want. It's more that I never really felt comfortable there. I got out as soon as I could – fleeing to the Gold Coast with my boyfriend when I was 21 years old because I thought life would be beautiful there. Well, it had to be better than southern Sydney, right?

Wrong. Well, maybe a little.

I have since travelled and lived in at least ten cities, yet it wasn't until recently that I really felt comfortable where I was – and it turned out it had nothing to do with the location, and everything to do with myself.

When you're little, you know no different than the experiences to which you are born. The truth is, I had no idea we lived on the wrong side of the tracks until I had started school. Another truth? Even the right side of the tracks in Rockdale suck. It's not a beautiful town, but that's not why it sucks. It's the energy - it's fast and unforgiving, and everyone is out for themselves. It's a multi-cultural hub with a rancid veil hovering over the town. It's all about drugs, gangs and illegal gaming houses - dictated by those with the most muscle. Okay, maybe I'm exaggerating a smidgen, but you get the picture.

I've heard of the old times when Rockdale had some charm, but those days were long gone even when I was a child. In the old days, the world was untarnished and charm was everywhere. I guess you could say it is still - that charm, like beauty, is in the eyes of the beholder. What

Rockdale lacks in charm, it makes up for with an ever-growing population. Maybe that's where the problem lies, because people aren't always charming. Nor are they always good.

But what is good, I hear you say.

Good is deep in your bones and ingrained in your soul. Good is empathy, and integrity, and treating others with respect and dignity. Good is your truth – it's in your words and actions, your thoughts and feelings, and it's the small voice whispering in your ear when confronted with choices. We can't always be good all of the time, but good is not killing a baby bird for pleasure.

One of the first and harshest lesson's involving the lack of good in humanity came when I was about five years old. Before that day, I knew not everyone was good all of the time – but I'd never witnessed cruelty firsthand. I guess that's why this day has imprinted upon my memory like an ugly stain.

Don't get me wrong, I was and still am no angel. I'm not always good. In fact, sometimes I like to be bad – in the best sense possible. The point is, I don't intentionally cause pain to another living being.

The school day was just beginning and it was raining. There was a bird's nest nestled deep along the eve of one of the school buildings and a baby bird had fallen to the ground – the asphalt playground.

My heart had leapt from my chest at the sight of the

little grey bird struggling helplessly in a puddle of rain water, and I remember being frightened for the creature. Before I had a chance to do anything, three older boys raced toward the chick. I was relieved. They would save the bird and hand it over to a teacher who would somehow return it to safety.

I was wrong.

Those boys huddled around the bird and began to laugh. Then the unthinkable – they started to take turns at stomping on the little grey bird as if it were better amusement than a Game & Watch Donkey Kong game (which by the way, I mastered – only a generation X would appreciate that fact).

My heart shattered and I screamed at those boys. They took no notice of me though. They just continued to stomp and laugh and I eventually had to turn away from the scene.

I'm not sure why those boys did that to the little helpless bird. I'm not saying they were or are bad people. Good people make wrong choices too. The incident played out within a matter of minutes, and it was over just as fast – little birds turn to mush pretty fast when stomped upon in the rain. But I cried for that bird. I cried in the playground, and I cried when I got home from school, and I cried when I awoke with the nightmares that had ensued.

One small bird showed me what it was to love and feel pain for something outside of myself and my family. One small bird showed me how to empathise, and taught me that people don't always do good things. And one small bird revealed something about myself that has remained with me all the days after – I am a bird.

You are too.

THE ART OF KISSING

"Oh, how she wanted to kiss those lips! Her quickened pulse felt like fire in her veins – she wanted to feel him now. Her eyes locked onto his as she closed the space between them, circling her hands around his neck and tangling her fingers in his hair as she crushed her lips against his."

~ excerpt from *Wildflower*, Kim Petersen

Okay, let's clear this up from the start – kissing is fun. No, more than that, kissing is bliss. Lips touch and tongues entwine in a beautiful language all of their own. You're drawn into a secret world known only to the two of you, and as the kiss deepens, you're pretty sure you could stay there forever. You might too, if you didn't need air.

Kissing. The world spins high, your pulse is a cackle of exquisite explosions, and the inducing body rush is enough to weaken your knees. Pleasurable chemicals are released – dopamine and adrenaline flood your being, and voila, you're in heaven, baby!

Kissing is probably underrated for the most part – the lingering looks and deep kisses wear off too quickly among couples that have been together for an extended period. It's a shame, a damned shame, because it's a proven fact that kissing is a de-stressor. Negative emotions shut down as the bonding hormone oxytocin is released, and kissing is found to decrease serum cholesterol. And let's not discount the physical benefit – we use around 30 muscles when kissing. That is toning, my friends! (So long Botox!)

I look over my kissing history with fond memories and cheesy grins. My lip trail began during those early school days playing kiss and catch with the boys. I learned how to run exceptionally fast back then. Oh yes, no way was I going to let a boy catch me. When my little legs failed and my heart was about to explode, I'd cheat and hide out in the school library, only to be sprung by my pursuers with nowhere to escape. Hiding behind teachers then became my game.

The kisses resulting upon capture in that childhood game were harmless little pecks. I'm not so sure what I was worried about. Maybe it was the prospect of being too close to sweaty boys. Arms would ensnare and hands grip my head like a vice before the incoming peck slammed against the cheek like a victorious stamp.

I changed schools during the 4th grade and graduated to more mature levels of kissing. Like, not. In that school, it was all about suggestive innuendo where the boys would say stuff like "I want to see your dictionary" and "I love eucalyptus". Or just stare until the blush crept up like raw beetroot. I mean – c'mon?

Seriously though, I'm no kissing expert, but I've experienced my fair share – from the downright WTF was that kind of kiss, to the soft romantic variety, to the euphoric depths of passion where too much is never enough. I've kissed boys, I've kissed men, and I've experienced the seductive lips of women. Believe me when I say, I understand why it's sooo nice to kiss women. But what about the first real kiss?

I'll tell you there were no stars soaring across the sky that night – no chemical rush to support the hype surrounding the art of the kiss. My pulse was flat and my stomach curled. I almost gave up on the notion of kissing then and there on that dark crowded dance floor during a Blue Light disco.

His name was Brandon. He was tall and solid, a whole lot of awkward and a whole lot of ginger. To be fair, it wasn't Brandon; it was his first kiss too, and he really was a sweetheart. I was fourteen and the thing was, all my friends were experts at the kissing game – all except me.

Every couple of months the NSW police department would organise a disco for the local teens. They'd set up a huge screen and feature video clips (MTV days). The music blasted, and the smoke machine worked overtime. Sometimes, they'd even have bands playing. It was awesome and we came in droves.

It was supposed to be a clean affair – no booze, no weed, no anything else. Naturally, we'd all figure our way around this little hiccup. Sneaky teens do rebel, and everyone would look forward to the next Blue Light disco. In its time, it was *the place to be.*

The problem? I was shy, but my friends thought it was about time I let someone plant a proper kiss on my inexperienced lips. And damn it, they were going to make it happen.

Poor Brandon. Poor me. It was a slobbery exchange of stiff lips and graceless tongues, and it lasted a few short moments before I excused myself and hid in a corner somewhere until I felt safe to face him again. We both decided we weren't into forced kissing. Well, I thought it was mutual decision and that was good enough for me.

The next time I summoned enough courage to press my lips against another's, it was my choice and my choosing. Thankfully, the path of getting down and saucy with cute boys, lips and tongues improved to hot exchanges that quickly backed up the whole kissing hype, and once mastered, I never looked back.

Whether it's something as simple as kissing, it's important to realise the need to trust our inner selves and take our cues from that voice within. I wasn't ready to kiss that boy that night. The act was forced and the result was disappointing, and I'd felt like I'd somehow failed. But when I was ready to kiss someone, it felt good and natural, and the experience unfolded as it should have, and I was left feeling positive.

You will never lead yourself astray if you take guidance from your inner-being and listen to your instincts. Now, what are you waiting for? Go pucker up and de-stress!

LOVE DOESN'T ALWAYS MEAN MONOGAMY

*T*hink back to your first relationship. Could you have been completely satisfied with remaining with that person forevermore? Could you have faced a lifetime of learning and growing from that first love? What about your second lover ... third?

While some of us are destined to discover true connection within that first relationship, more often than not this isn't the case. By true connection, I am referring to the kind of bonds that trigger inner growth on the essential levels – emotionally; spiritually; sexually; soulfully.

Complete fusion.

These are the qualities vital to propel and shift us into

expansion as we move through life. Relational aspects that continue to flourish and deepen as the connection matures – rare bonds established on a soul level destined to rattle our senses, ignite change and show us deep love.

There are all kinds of love - Self-love; affectionate and playful love; familiar and enduring love.

Unconditional love.

It is through experiencing love that we learn how to give and receive love. We learn important qualities like empathy, gratitude and compassion. Each connection brings inner growth and teaches us what it means to bond and share selflessly.

To love and be loved is our ultimate purpose during our lifetimes.

It is strange how western society in particular has managed to erect invisible boundaries and rules around the concept of love, and in the process, thwarting the true meaning behind love and connection.

Real love is freedom.

To believe we embark on a lifetime to experience just one

significant mate is delusional. Pepper Schwartz, a professor of sociology at the University of Washington in Seattle said: "Monogamy is invented for order and investment – but not necessarily because it's natural."

If humans were truly monogamous creatures, we would behave like geese – stick with our first mates and take none thereafter; even after the death of a spouse. There would be no divorce or second marriages, and there would be no tallying up the U.S. average of 7.2 sexual partners found in a recent Superdrug survey.

While the idea of committing to and sharing our lives with someone we love is a natural state to experience, so too is the falling ins and outs of relationships. In other words, not all relationships are designed or destined to last a lifetime.

In fact, most are not. It is natural for us to form and honor important connections as those souls move through our experience. Yet, we are on a continuous learning path and therefore, are supposed to be reaching for more in order to expand and evolve to higher states of being.

We do this through relationships and connections.

Relationships are the springboard for life-lessons and

growth. Some relationships reach their peak before the connection plateaus to a place that no longer challenges us to grow and evolve into a better human being.

It is all about personal and spiritual growth and less about societal expectations and the pre-conceived ideals surrounding marriages. We are taught that it is wrong to fall in love with someone else when married or involved in a long-term relationship. We are made to feel ashamed for experiencing deep feelings for someone other than our spouse.

This school of thought is limiting and self-serving. It doesn't take into account how we change with time and attract new situations into our lives. It doesn't acknowledge that it is natural for us to encounter, bond and share connections with other people who cross our paths for the purpose of expanding love and further propelling us into higher awareness. And it does not equate to love without condition.

Life happens.

Sometimes, we are presented with a bombshell in the form of a special connection despite our current circumstances. I have listened to folks speak about how we get to choose who we love, when in reality, the opposite is true.

When real love touches our lives and imprints upon our soul, we have as much control over our feelings as we do the weather. We cannot control who captures our hearts and when; we cannot account for the appearance of those deep soul connections. That is one of life's most beautiful mysteries.

In fact, it is common that we cannot be truly ready to experience the greatest love of our lives until we have journeyed through other relationships that serve to prepare us for the ultimate connection.

I am by no means condoning cheating in the self-gratifying, adulterous sense. Nor promoting disrespect or hedonistic behavior.

What I mean is that often we make commitments and promises that hold true in the moment. Yet, signing a marriage contract doesn't always account for the inevitable transformation bound to happen with maturity. Existing commitments cannot foresee detours in a person's feelings or predict the future.

From the moment we are born we are learning, evolving and experiencing the world for the sole purpose of personal growth and soul lessons. Whether we acknowledge the fact that we are much more than our fleshy tombs becomes highly personal and reflective of where we are in terms of spiritual advancement.

When we are able to step back long enough to recognize connection for its true purpose, we may grasp the notion that nothing about relationships should encompass feelings of control or possession over another being - marital contract or not.

It is then we can see that relating and bonding with another person is about opening the heart and learning how to love unconditionally. It is the ability to allow your mate the freedom to experience their portion of life without imposing your will, insecurities or underlying desires upon their journey.

That is the true meaning of unconditional love – to love unselfishly and without placing a set of restrictions along with your affections or companionship. Unfortunately, very few of us strive to practice this kind of love.

The institution of marriage is a somewhat outdated notion in the grand scheme of things. Particularly when considering the advancement of humanity, and especially when contemplating the natural state of relations between the first humans to inhabit the earth who had very little use for marriage.

It is presumed that early males and females had sex with many partners, with the initial formations of marriages emerging around climate change and food - a richer meat-based diet meant that babies were born earlier requiring more care from their mothers. Before that, mothers were able to gather fruit and nuts whilst caring for their infants.

These may not have been marriages in the way that we think of marriages today, but couples in this period would probably have stayed together for about three or four years before parting ways. Perhaps it is no coincidence that this is exactly the length of time at which divorce rates peak in modern day marriages.

It was during this era that marriages became a union between two people and recognized by the community. Agriculture tied people to the land, meaning that at the end of the four-year period couples were less inclined to separate, choosing to work as a unit to feed and care for the children they produced.

The creation of marriage as a legal contract between men and women came into being over time as communities settled on what was a normal way for them to organize a family and then condense that normalcy into law.

Laws were created that gave men assurance that the children they were raising were their own; women that their husband would not leave them destitute.

So, the real origin of marriage evolved from the biological desire of both men and women to see their children survive, and until recently had less to do with love.

We are fast to claim each other forevermore. We typically thrive on co-dependency and are quick to pass judgment, point fingers and damn the one for following their heart should love come calling unexpectedly.

We seek to own, take commitment and twist it into something unnatural until it becomes a liability when our natural state of being is the opposite – **real love is the opposite.**

Love is as mysterious and as beautiful as the meaning of life. Love doesn't know restrictions – gender, age, geographical or race differences. Love doesn't always recognize the institution of marriage.

It is an illusion to believe we have control over another human being within a marriage or otherwise. It is a farce to believe we can prevent another from falling in love with someone else. All we are able to do is to practice being the best possible version of ourselves within any given moment – including when a relationship begins to no longer serve our greater needs, and especially when facing a straying spouse.

How we handle those high-level situations are what defines us as human beings.

Our greater needs are always about love and experiencing love in its highest form. Letting go of stale relationships is a part of the human experience. Allowing a relationship to end gracefully rather than bitterly is a part of love – caring for yourself enough to take the higher-road and knowing that all things unfold for your own growth and well-being as well as that of others.

Love only knows freedom and expression - It is

acceptance and the ability to see past the blinders, the ego and the societal expectations on what constitutes a proper relationship. Love is allowing someone to be who they want to be, even when it hurts. **Real love is truly freedom.**

TRIBES

I'd never been the outgoing, make-friends-easy type. For as long as I can remember, I have been shy around new people. I was the little kid hiding behind my mother's skirt if a stranger dared smile my way. Should an adult so much as uttered a word to me back then, all kinds of inner turmoil would ensue. I would literally clam up, tongue-tied and nervous, while trying to figure out how to actually speak without sounding like an idiot. I would later discover my Myer Briggs personality type, which happened to explain a lot. Turns out, it's normal for INTP's to feel odd, because well, underneath all that cool exterior, we are oddballs at heart and so easily misunderstood.

Not only did I have an introverted personality to contend with, I also had a torrent of self-esteem/confidence issues deeply ingrained in my psyche ever since I can remember. In short, the self-confidence was lacking somewhere beyond my feet. It would take me a lot of years to yank it back where it belonged – even then, the struggles are ongoing. Perhaps it is because I come from a long-line of introverts (father's side of the family).

My father has to be the most introverted person I've ever known – you want reserved, quiet, non-speaking individuals? I've got plenty lined up around here. Let's just say, dinner conversation wasn't a big thing in my childhood. Never-the-less, introversion is a whole other subject I'll definitely talk about in the future. For now, we're hitting the tribe topic – friends.

Despite my shortcomings in the making-friends-department, by the time I reached 16 years of age, I managed to eventually surround myself with a handful of gems. Genuine people I will never forget. I guess being an introvert, you're able to sift along the side-lines, scraping through the constant noise and chaos in the world and eventually attract the stickers – the diamonds in the ruff, the real-deal. In case you didn't get it, I'm talking about the bona fide, sincere folks that live with integrity in their hearts and breathe the air of loyalty.

I found them. Or they found me. Either way, the tribe was established and we were in it together through thick and thin. Apart from two close school friends, the members in my tribe were about three to four years older than me. Looking back, I think the age difference made all the difference – they had cars (yippee!). No, seriously, the difference in age reflected in their take on the world. These guys and gals were thoughtful visionaries, penetrating the future with a contemplative flare I admired.

Every weekend, we'd grab our gear, and our gear, before we'd all pile into those cars and head west toward the Hawkesbury River – a 120 kilometre stretch of water that eventually flows into the Tasman Sea. Once there, we'd find our little weekend hub in the form of a camp ground by the river. A quiet spread of countryside nestled in the green valleys of Lower Portland. I can tell you though, the rolling, serene landscape was no more following the arrival of our tribe. Especially come night.

By day, we were slaves to the river. The speed boats were lowered carefully down the eroded ramps and into the water. The flashy wetsuits were adorned, the water skis dusted off for another run, and we'd hit that water like tomorrow might never come. Then, the sun would begin to shift over the horizon, giving way to a more chilled vibe involving camp fires, Led Zeppelin and Pink Floyd. You can fill in the rest for yourself.

Good times. We've all had them – memories that impress somewhere in your brain matter and lend you that nostalgic smile every now then. Recalling the good stuff is like the sweetest candy for your soul, and I am grateful for every single piece that indulges me. Those are memories I'll cherish for all of time. Even the ones that were born from horror. You see, hanging out with people and enjoying great experiences is awesome, but it isn't until the shit hits the fan that you realise the strong bonds you have formed with the people in your life. That's when friends transcend beyond the standard friendship. That's when you realise the love that exists between you.

It was New Year's Eve 1991 and I was 17 years old with no parents in sight (Hellloooo, Freedom). It was those weird-ass summer months in Australia, you know, those strange days that begin around Christmas and last until the school year resumes. I was staying on my own in my home with my boyfriend and my little brother.

We'd decided to attend a party at a nearby beach pub beer garden – minus the little brother, of course. The usual players came along – my beloved tribe, as well as a whole lot of other people I didn't know. The night passed in the standard New Year celebratory fashion – the bourbons went down faster than you could say "I want another drink", the music caused some hips to swing, and the conversations were utterly intense. In a good way. I think. I could say we saw the new year in gracefully, but I'd be lying.

By the time the hours grew thin and we made the moves to go home, things got a little out of whack. There's that threshold with booze – the moment when it all seems to flood your system at once and control becomes a faded inkling beyond your grasp. Before you jump to conclusions, I'm not actually talking about myself. It was the boyfriend. Way too much beer and whatever else might've found its way down his cake hole that night, and things got bad pretty fast.

I'm not going to go into the nitty-gritty of it all, but the scene ended with lost car/house keys, broken glass and vanished precious jewellery, an enormous amount blood, emergency surgery and tears – buckets of them. By the night's end, I was sitting in a hospital waiting room waiting for the doctors to bring news of my boyfriend's micro-surgery and watching the sun rise.

Meh. Shit happens.

Actually, at the time, it was pretty traumatic shit and the experience left me feeling numb, lost and alone, and totally out of my depth. There were no parents around to mop up the mess. Nobody to take the lead and make it alright. I was 17 and going home to an empty apartment stained with gallons of blood and shattered glass. With no keys to unlock the front door, no less.

As it turned out, that couldn't have been farther from the truth. Remember those friends I was rambling on about earlier?

Yeah. Hell. Yeah.

They swept in beneath me like the feathers of angel wings, cocooning all around me. It was them that had all the keys replaced, them that picked me up and took me to the hospital every day, them that cleaned out the apartment and took me to the location to painstakingly search for the gold chain and pendants that were so sentimental to me. Them that made sure I was okay each moment of every day until the ordeal passed.

As I write these words, I can't help but feel the warmth trickling through my being. I will always love those people. They are my people, even when the years stretch between us. The power of true friendship is an all-encompassing journey not to be taken for granted. Treasure those that honour you and appreciate the layers they bring to your life – sweet soul candy can never be underestimated.

And yes, with the help of my friends, we'd found each and every little gold charm that'd I'd lost on a shadowy street when the world darkened and sanity was temporality misplaced. I still have them.

GETTING REAL

Who Am I?

Have you ever sat down and silently pondered that question? I mean, really allowed the thought to seep into your consciousness to the point you're confronted with your deepest truths. What you see and acknowledge when you strip the layers can be rather unsettling at first, but when you push past the flesh and bone, and give your undivided attention to your essence, the feelings that erupt are indescribable.

It's at this moment you come into the full realisation that you are nothing that the outer-world sees, and *everything* that lives and thrives within you.

In January 2007 I walked out on a life I'd been living for over a decade. It was a life that flourished beneath the oppressive hands of brutality and domination. I had left that world behind with no inkling of who I was, who I could be, or indeed, if I was even worthy of happiness.

In that marriage, I wasn't permitted to be myself. Every remark, thought, idea and action I'd made was inevitably met with harsh criticism and condemnation, and sometimes, a hard slap on the face. I was living on the edge of my nerves, and slowly suffocating as a result. My then husband had no idea who I really was, and he had no interest in discovering what I could offer as an individual either.

I believe even the most difficult relationships exist solely for our personal growth. Sometimes it might feel just the opposite, though. What can you possibly learn about yourself when living under such repressive conditions? Surely those relationships hinder your growth?

Maybe. I guess.

I once knew of an elderly couple that lived in my neighbourhood. They were widely known around town because the old husband severely abused his wife. The abuse had been going on for decades, through the raising of their family and the eventual arrival of grandchildren. Nobody could understand why that little old lady stayed with her monster of a husband. He was cruel and unjust, and he treated her worse than their family dog.

The thing that stuck out in my mind the most, though, was that when they drove past in their car, the husband would force his wife to sit in the back seat. She wasn't worthy enough to claim the front seat beside him. In his mind, she was beneath him. So, he'd drive his car down the street with his ego belted in, and his thin frail wife hunched behind him in the back seat. It was plain to see that this old man had accomplished his objective – he'd broken her spirit.

How does that make you feel? That a human being could view another in such a derogatory light? That a person compiled of the same flesh and blood as you and me could dare think he was a superior being and squish the light from another?

I'll tell you how it makes me feel – saddened. For both of them. There is nothing more tragic than for one person to limit another human being. Such mind-control towards a sensitive person can limit that person for years and can even be compared to murder – spirit murder.

When another person treats you in that way, it is never about you and everything about the way the perpetrator feels about themselves and their view of the world. It's what you choose to accept to be true that informs your experiences. Can you imagine the internal torment involved in such circumstances? I can. I've lived it.

That old lady had suffered at the hands of her husband her entire married life and eventually accepted that to be true for her experience. She felt that she deserved nothing more from life. She was too broken, too hopeless, and too unloved to act on any impulse to change her life, even if she had wanted to. And I'm not talking about the love she didn't feel from her husband, I'm talking about self-love.

Yet, the life that woman had accepted to be true for herself was the driving force behind the life I eventually rejected. It was her slouching image sitting in the back seat of the car that played in my mind for twelve long years. It was the same image that I vowed not to become. Sometimes, a chosen life of despair has a profound ripple effect far greater than what we realise. For that woman's heartache and horrific experience, I can only wish her love and give gratitude for the impact it had over mine.

Still, I did not go unscathed, and entered a new life without really knowing who I was or what I wanted. It wasn't long after that that I felt an underlying pull towards the divinity. When the moments grow silent and stillness is all around, and you are alone, eventually you have to face yourself and travel a path towards the truth.

The future spread out before me like an uncarved road I couldn't quite envision, and although there were often times that I felt scared, I chose to trust in the part of myself that was real – my soul, my essence. It was the part that connected me to something far greater than myself.

Well, I figured I had no choice really, and I did so with a sense of excitement. In those early years of awakening to new ideas and self-awareness, I didn't understand what I was feeling all of the time, but when I discovered new revelations, it was like pure bliss for my soul. I could sense my soul rejoicing as I evolved. I remember opening books and reading the text, and revelling in the euphoric buzz that would ensue as the remnants of the truth resonated within me.

I look back now and I realise I had been standing on the threshold of what would unfold as my own personal spiritual journey. And with every fibre of my being, I understand I couldn't have reached that level of self-evolution and self-awareness without experiencing the pain and angst of abusive relationships.

I chose to grow from those experiences. I chose myself, and I chose to seek answers to the questions that had always plagued me – who am I, really? I knew there was more, much more, and I wasn't satisfied with the dense 3D version we face here on the earth plane.

So, what is real?

Real is love, real is what is inside of you.

I am love, and so are you.

THE UNREAL

"What is real?"
"That is real which never changes."
~ Ancient spiritual avatar from the book *Wishes Fulfilled* by Wayne Dyer.

*D*uring a recent conversation with my mother, she asked me what I considered to be materialistic. I felt a slight surge of delight ripple through me as I gazed towards the rolling green ranges that spread out from my home on the other side of the valley. They are the same peaks I regularly consult. Yes, I talk to the mountains as well as the stars and the ocean, because it is among those natural elements that I feel most anchored to the mystery of life.

The mystery of life has nothing to do with anything I own, or how much money I have in my bank account. I took a breath and smiled. I was ready to engage; this was my kind of talk.

Materialism.

The word instantly conjures images of money-oriented people who are excessively concerned about gathering material possessions – and yes, it's exactly what the word implies. According to Madonna we do live in a material world, right?

Look around. Just about everything you see is tangible. If you can touch it, squeeze it and mould it, it must be real. The more money you can accumulate, the more of the real you can gather. The more of the real you can collect and own, the more you become real. Well, you must be real if you own things, and I'm more real because mine is bigger than yours.

Bigger. Better. Bullshit.

I've never measured my success or my self-worth on material possessions, even when I was younger and surrounded by people that liked nothing more than to compare their earthly possessions or talk non-stop about money. I've never understood. Honestly, I could not care less if your shoes are worth $500 or what kind of car you drive, or how big your house is.

Granted, it's nice to have cool things to play with – I get that, I do. I feel there is absolutely nothing wrong with wanting the stuff you want. After all, that's why we come here – to sift through our experiences; desire, want and create what we want, and learn as we walk the path. Of course, I want things for myself and my family. But for me, it's the intention behind the desire that differs from the materialistic sense.

I'll be honest, I do want success. I want financial freedom, I want to travel and explore parts of the world that beckon me, and I want to live in a home on the edge of a cliff overlooking the ocean. I would love to own a secluded cabin nestled deep in the woods too. Is that being materialistic?

Maybe. To some. Especially for those who might be getting a little uncomfortable reading this article and are beginning to think I'm being hypocritical.

My desires are fuelled by something other than physical comfort and wanting the biggest and the best. I want what I want because we *do* live in a world where money is necessary in order to survive, and fundamental to be able to expand our experiences.

More than anything, I want to expand, experience and savour what the world has to offer. I want to visit sacred caves in Colorado. I want to travel to places off the beaten track, be among Tibetan monks, make love at Niagara Falls, and experience diverse cultures because that is the kind of stuff that will enrich my soul. I choose the home by the sea and a cabin in the woods because that's where I feel most connected with earth's energy. That's where I can breathe and just be when I need time away from the world.

I say this, yet at the same time it's so important to get away from the importance of money, and to view it as only a means of exchange. But how do you achieve that? – By working to shed the cultural bonds that have been conditioned in us since birth; by dying to the ideals and values that measure us on a materialistic basis and reinventing our perspectives, and perhaps surrendering to a new outlook that money and material possessions are not real.

The answer I gave my mother was simple – I consider anything that cannot be taken with you upon your physical death to be materialistic. Anything.

This is where it gets interesting for me because I'm not only talking about material possessions. I'm talking about anything that isn't really you – Ego. Reputation. Beliefs. Personality. Values. Hatred. Fame. Accolades. Emotions. Body.

I'm not saying these attributes are unimportant, or as important as you want them to be, but each of those qualities change. All these unseen influences make up who we are and how we view the world during our lifetimes, but you won't be taking your reputation along with you when you cark it. Nobody on the other side is going to care how many awards you won.

At the end of your life, all you get to take is your soul

and the growth fostered during the experience of your lifetime. And I'll tell you this for free; it's only about love – how much you learned from it, and how much you were able to give and receive.

If that is real that never changes, then real can only be your spirit or soul.

What is real is love.

GREENHORN

"Opinions are like assholes, everybody has one."
~ Dirty Harry.

The first time I heard those words spoken wasn't during a screening of a Clint Eastwood flick. No blue-eyed, hard-nosed, convention defying Harry Callahan strutting with his Smith & Wesson revolver lit up my screen and branded my ears with that sentence for the first time. Far from it. I was twenty and it had been during a showing of the Nazi symbol firmly tattooed on the brawny arm of a bikie greenhorn.

Maybe I'd had one too many bourbons that night, or maybe I'd grown comfortable enough around these new friends to finally express myself a little. But then again, perhaps it was just when I was confronted by a symbol that to me represented fascism, dictatorship and the murder of around six million people that I had trouble taming the instant revulsion swirling in my belly. And there it was, flung out in the open before I could catch it – my opinion.

The words started to roll over my tongue, and at each unsatisfactory answer, I probed even more. Suddenly, I wanted to know why the bikie beefcake wore that symbol on his arm as if it were a prized medal, and more importantly, I wanted to know *how* he could choose to believe in such an atrocity.

And he wanted me to "shut the f**k up".

I have an asshole, you see.

Those were the days when I was introduced to a new world of long whiskers, leather jackets and hot motorbikes. I know what you're thinking, but before romanticised visions of *Sons of Anarchy* flood your mind, I'll stop you right there. There were no super-hot males swaggering around in tight jeans and fitted shirts. And certainly, no Jax Teller straddling a shiny Harley-Davidson and beckoning me to cosy up behind him before whisking me off into the sunset.

Uh-uh. Not even close.

But that's not why that scene fast became a fleeting memory for me. I stuck it out for a few months because my boyfriend had decided they were his new tribe. To be fair, some of them *were* his childhood friends. But in the end, I discovered it was a world in which I didn't belong.

It wasn't that they were bad people. Although none of them remotely resembled Jax from the above-mentioned notorious biker series, for the most part, they were fun to hang out with and quite accommodating. There were no qualms when it came to sharing, and I have to admit, they knew how to party. And party hard they did. I'd even made a friend among them. She was one of the girlfriends. She was blonde and nice, in a rough-around-the-edges kind of way, and she took a liking to me.

After a while, though, she was banished from her biker-girlfriend position, and cast aside for the next in line. She piled her belongings into her car and to my surprise, stopped by my house on the way out of town to give me my first dreamcatcher because she said I was the nicest person she'd met in Sydney. Another surprise. I mean, I knew she liked me but to be the *nicest* person she'd met in Sydney? I was honoured.

Then I remembered her choice of company.

Wait – was that another opinion flung out across my keyboard?

Well, I do have an asshole remember, and I'm betting the last time you checked, you do too. In all seriousness, I didn't think more or less of that particular group of people. They were no different to me, and free to express their opinions and beliefs as much as the next person, even if the Nazi symbol had offended me at the time.

Actually, the part that had upset me the most during that interaction was when the bikie greenhorn responded with the phrase so famously spoken by Clint Eastwood in the movie *The Dead Pool*. I remember blushing and feeling embarrassed. I had no idea how to react, and suddenly felt self-conscious. I guess he had accomplished his intention, because yeah, I shut up pretty fast following that remark. And something else occurred to me – not everyone wanted to hear my opinion, and nor was it necessary for me to share it.

Opinions. Unless you're a Buddhist monk, most of us can't get through life without forming them, believing in them and living according to them. Hell, even Buddhist monks live according to their beliefs, right?

They are the threads of thoughts drawn from our experiences, our cultural, societal and academic backgrounds, and family heritage, and are strung together to eventually inform our belief systems.

We have all kinds of belief systems, too – religious and spiritual beliefs, political beliefs, philosophical and ideological, and the list goes on to eventually settle in the core of your being after you have sifted through it all and decided to adhere to a set of beliefs that feel right to you.

But what are beliefs and opinions really?

Practised thoughts. Practise a thought enough and it

will become your reality. I could say I believed the sight of that Nazi tattoo offended me – until it didn't. Until I realised that by allowing the outer conditions of my world to influence my reactions and feelings, that I was really giving power to circumstances and conditions outside of myself.

I'm not saying I had a complete about-face and now advocate the heinous actions of the Nazis and what would result as the holocaust. Quite the contrary. But I *am* saying that you can never escape the opinions and beliefs of others, and you're not always going to agree or like what you see or hear. You can, however, choose how you react to those situations, and you can choose not to allow the opinions of others influence your self-esteem and self-worth.

Do I always get this right?

Hell no.

I still get hurt and feel emotional pain, and sometimes have fleeting moments of loss of control. Only now, it is the people that I *love* that can stir my most inner emotions. **I don't give that power away too easily these days**, and even then, it has its limitations because I remind myself that I cannot pin my happiness, the outcome of my life, or my self-worth on anyone other than myself.

People will always have opinions, feel the need to share them and judge. You can't stop it – even in yourself at times. But when I hear someone judging another person or impressing their opinions about them, or even when I feel the urge to pass judgement on another myself, I recall the words of Matt Kahn when he said, "May the person judging be the next in line for love."

At the end of the day, that's all we can do – qualify judgement with love and move on.

Move on with love.

GIVE AND TAKE

My mother has been catapulted into a new existence since my stepfather passed away in early 2018. She has had to learn how to stand on her own two feet for the first time in her life. She's had to work out how to pump her own petrol, pay the bills and handle finances. She's learned how to interact with industry people, negotiate deals and assert herself in the world. Mostly, she's had no choice but to sift through the many layers of herself and discover who she is without her husband.

It's in those small, quiet hours alone that you cannot hide from yourself. Those are the moments when the truth finds you. When you can no longer run from who you are. She's not into being alone. I am. I can happily spend hours at a time without interacting with people. Introspection is my thing – almost to a fault.

This might sound weird, but I love thinking, reflecting and delving into the deepest zones of my mind. I can easily become lost in a world of my own making; analyzing, day dreaming, over-thinking situations and playing futuristic conversations and scenes in my head.

Ah, cerebral heaven. Is it wrong that I would rather spend my time in this reflection mode than engage in meaningless, no-point conversations?

This is something else my mother has had to learn since she's been on her own – me.

Okay, I admit that my preference to living in my own head might sound a little aloof or unfriendly, but it's really not. It comes down to need and sanity. I *need* space – lots of space. It's the way I process the world, my life and feelings. She doesn't understand. If I'm denied this reflection time for extended periods, I tend to get irritable and edgy. Maybe even a little grouchy.

The same is true when it hits a certain time of the evening and I see one of my kids trouncing around the house. I could never understand how some folks allow their children to stay up till all hours – *argh!* Give me a break; I need "adult time". You know, to get my reflection on and chill without looking at a chicken.

My mother likes to talk ... a lot. To the point it drives me crazy. She likes to tell me about people – what they're doing, where they're going and snippets of conversations. Suffering, that's what that is. I don't want to know why so-

and-so is going to Timbuktu and how the old buddy is getting the whatchamacallit. In the politest sense possible, I don't give a fuck.

It gets worse. Well, from an introvert's perspective. She wants to know stuff that I know too. About people. A few days ago, she asked me about a friend of mine that is planning to move farther north. He and his wife are considering an island life.

Mother took it upon herself to have a rant about this decision – farther north means cyclonic weather. Island life means …. erm …. the probability of Bogans. I didn't understand why she would bother wasting brain power on other people's life choices; she really meant that shit. I was utterly baffled.

Then came the question:
"Which island?"

Which island? Was she serious? Does she not know me?

I responded with a shrug and the truth.

"I don't know; my brain doesn't retain that information, mum."

"In other words, you don't give a fuck?"

Ding, ding! Now we're getting somewhere. She really said that by the way. Don't tell her I told you though because she's truly a lady and we all know that ladies don't talk that way. Apart from the lady typing these words. And yes, I am a lady. Particularly when it suits. I might be *elegantly* corrupting her a smidge.

Elegantly. There's a word. It just rolls off your tongue, does it not?

A little intel for the word nerds:

Elegant origins: *Meaning "characterized by refined grace" is from 1520s. Latin elegans originally was a term of reproach, "dainty, fastidious": the notion of "tastefully refined" emerged in classical Latin. Related: Elegantly.*

2019 and the word "fuck" can be *elegantly* inserted in most annotations. Everybody is aware of the versatility this word holds. In fact, it's one of the most resourceful words ever created. Its use can convey happiness, sadness, anger, disbelief, arousal, excitement and confusion among other things. But did you know there's another multi-layered word used in Australia that is just as if not more adaptable?

Hint: It rhymes with runt.

There are all kinds of …. umm …. "runts" here – cheeky ones, sick ones, mad ones, good and bad ones. There are "runts" all over the place in this sun-blessed country. You can't avoid them, but I try to steer clear of the crazy ones.

As much as Australians have taken this word beneath their laid-back *"she'll be right"* wings, I avoid using it like the plague because I fucking hate it. My mother might say it's not very elegant.

I walk in the mornings when the sun rises. Sometimes, I run. Mumma-bear sleeps at my place at least one night a week and joins me for these dawn outings when she's here. She won't run though. I'm not sure if it's because running is a bit much for her at her age or if it's because when she tried it once, I laughed so hard that I almost fell over. I can't even begin to describe the sight of her arms flapping around in her white sweater like a baby penguin chasing its mother.

Entertainment. Some might even say cheap thrills, but who's listening and who actually gives a fuck? Apparently, and according to her, I run elegantly. Who knew that was even a thing?

Told you I was a lady.

Jokes aside, it's not that I don't care about people – even the crazy "runts" from time to time. On the contrary, I care very much about the people that matter to me. That doesn't mean I concern myself with the nuts and bolts of their lives or judge their choices and motivations. I'm sure they know what they're doing. Somewhat. Who really knows what they're doing, anyhow?

Show me someone who has it all figured out and I'll show you a pair of earbud cords that never become tangled. They don't exist, at least not in my world. Have you ever cursed those damned cords? I do. Frequently. They always seem to knot in the most intricate way when you need to get them in your ear quick-smart. They're the times when I might be inclined to use the word that rhymes with runt.

Psyche.

Maybe one day I will figure it all out. Till then, my mother is still learning that I'm nothing like her and that I don't have the capacity to engage in a continuous stream of phatic conversation. And I'll keep trying to pretend to be interested in Bob, Sue and Whathisname for just that little bit longer because in the end, relationships are about giving and taking, even when you don't give an elegant fuck.

LIVING FROM THE HEART

There are two types of people in the world: those who hang their toilet paper rolls in an over position, and those who hang it in the under position. You can tell a lot about a person about the way they hang their ass-napkins. According to Dr Gilda Carle, *"People who roll over are more dominant than those who roll under."*

Carle went so far as to suggest that you could use this information to see if you're compatible with new partners.

There's an idea. Perhaps those looking for love should add this information to their online dating profiles or use it as an opening line when someone in a crowded bar catches their eye.

"Hey baby, do you take it under or over?"

Gasp.

"How dare you!"

"Nah, you got it all wrong, sugar. I mean your shit sheets? Do you like the roll under or over?"

"Err ... I'm an under-roller."

Brows raise. Hands wave furiously while backing up.

"Oh ... you're one of those psychopathic weirdos who like to make it hard on yourself. Sorry ... I'm only looking for over-rolling ladies."

Have you ever switched the hang of a toilet roll when using the bathroom at someone else's house? I have. I'm guessing by now you may have worked out that I'm an over-roller. Yep, I take my toilet tissue over and my eggs over-easy please. It just makes sense. Why make it harder on yourself?

Speaking of harder, I'm wondering if those submissive under-rollers are among the touchier beings in our society. Think about it, hanging a toilet roll in the under position is awkward if not miserable. Clearly it takes an under-person sadist to enjoy unrolling the paper in the wrong direction.

Some people are broadminded. Others are not. Maybe there is a correlation between "under-rollers" and sensitivity, or "under-rollers" and social difficulties. Rolling the toilet paper under may indicate core issues about uptight behaviors and attitudes.

Of course, this is just harmless speculation and I'm (partly) joking (under-rollers, lower your pitchforks and lighten up). But while we're on the subject of rigidness, why not explore the difference between broadmindedness and small-mindedness a little?

Societal structure and cultural conditioning help to define our values, beliefs and ethical systems, ultimately shaping the way we perceive ourselves in the world. Yet, if we take a group of people from the same community with similar upbringings and look closer, we soon realize the vast differences between them, including their outlook on life.

Personality plays a significant role. We're all unique in that sense. Friedman and Rosenman conceptualized a set of behavioral responses collectively known as Type A Behavior Pattern.

Their research showed that people with the Type A personality behaviors were more competitive, ambitious, impatient and aggressive than those exhibiting Type B behaviors who are said to be relaxed, non-competitive individuals. And just in case you're wondering, apparently Type A's favor the over-roll.

The Myer-Briggs Type Indicator (MBTI) is an extensive, research-based adaptation of Carl Jung's psychological types theory encompassing 16 personality types. And while they act as useful reference points to understand your unique personality, it's worth keeping in mind the human experience is complex and cannot fully be defined within such narrow perimeters.

For instance, I fall into the INPT personality type on

the MBTI. Much of the traits attributed to this type are relatable to my personality, and yet I cannot completely rest my identity as an INPT.

In other words, I won't allow a set of personality-based indicators define who I am as a person. I am much more than a list of indicative words in a study. I have deep layers, intricate fabric and human experiences that have accumulated to make up who I am.

The above-mentioned factors definitely play a part in forming a person's mindset tendencies, but in the end the difference between a fixed mindset and an open mindset comes down to personal choice.

In each moment we choose how we want to see the world and our reactions toward it. *We choose our perspectives* and therefore, the empathy we demonstrate toward others in any given moment.

Small fragments of time exist between our responses. Each time we are confronted by a situation is another opportunity to choose our behavior. Poor reactions are indicative of the emotions we have toward ourselves.

In other words, when someone treats you like garbage, it says more about them than it does you. Those poor responses are usually symbolic of a fixed mindset and the emotions driving it.

As we mature, so too do our hearts. Forms of love exist to teach and cultivate the rich stuff like empathy, compassion, connection and courage.

We begin to learn patterns of love early on through family relationships. We thrive and grow through our love of life, forming friendships that teach us about respect, compromise and integrity. Then, we are confronted with the ultimate heart-lessons through romantic love and connection.

> *"These experiences of love and expressions of love drive this center to transform our whole being to greater states of awareness as the heart closes to heal, transform and reopen to yet another love. This is how your heart transforms you, moves you to fulfill your passion and challenges your courage to go deeper and quest longer. This is transformation through cycles of rebirth of your spirit."* – Rose Carey

It is through the wonderful journey of our hearts and love-lessons that we learn tolerance, kindness and the ability to open our minds as we open our hearts to others. It is our hearts that provide the gateway to an open mind and not our personalities or cultural backgrounds. Our hearts are powerful enough to embrace new ways of thinking and being, and smash away invisible rigid boundaries that imprison us. It is through our hearts that our worldview is shaped.

Choosing to live from the heart center means we choose benevolence over self-centeredness, love over fear, tolerance over narrow-mindedness. Through our heart center we realize that we are much more than the "physical" self as we become aware of our divinity. And whether you are an under-roller or over-roller in the shit sheet department, that my friends is what makes the difference between a fixed mindset or an open mindset.

How open is your heart?

ROCK, STARS & SIGNS

"I'm part of you
You're part of me
There's nothing said
That cannot be undone"
– Lyrics from *I'm Just a Man*.

Songwriters: Michael Hutchence, Andrew Farriss

Michael Hutchence. In my opinion, he was one of the greatest rock stars of all time. Indeed, he was among the last true rock stars of his era, right up there with Bono, Billy Idol, Axel Rose and Mick Jagger. He possessed the right amount of magnetism, mystique and recklessness, and his stage presence was unbelievably dynamic. When he strutted out on that stage, the world became a faded memory, swallowed by the charismatic guy crooning a tune and seducing the crowd with the deliberate grind of his hips. Qualities of a rock star.

Some say Michael was sex-on-a-stick. I couldn't agree more. Somehow, that man had more sex appeal entwined around his little finger than Brad Pitt starring in *Legends of the Fall*.

Hold on a sec, I'm recalling the female sighs drifting above the cinema during a screening of that flick and I'm thinking that might be a slight exaggeration. Regardless, the man wasn't ashamed of his sexuality. He owned it and flaunted it accordingly.

Sigh.

He was definitely no *prude*. I think he must have appreciated the yin and yang between the sexes because let's face it, he was never short on "yin" company, and he was probably smart enough to nurture those precious connections too.

Yin: *the divine female principle of the universe.*

Do you ever notice the signs the universe throws your way? Sometimes those signs can be subtle little hints to let you know you are on the right path. Other times, they're like a freight train smacking you in the face till you laugh like a crazy person and yell at the cosmos to *"just stop already"*.

Last Saturday I drove my daughter to her boyfriend's house before picking up some lunch at the local shops. I was literally on the road for about twenty-five minutes during which time I saw "yin" five times.

Five times, people. *What the f**k is that all about?*

Some kind of cosmic prank? Either that, or I think there might be a sudden influx of "yin" infecting car number plates around here. Gets even better. I arrived home to find my other daughter had sketched a picture for me, and low and behold it was the Yin-Yang symbol.

I literally gasped when she waved in front of me.

"Do you like it?"

"Uh-yeah. It's beautiful, pussycat." Slight pause, then. "Why did draw that?"

Big brown eyes blink up at me with a shrug.

"Because I like it and I wanted to."

Duh.

"Do you know what it means?"

Nose crinkle. Cherry lips twist. Eyes narrow over me.

"Nah. I just saw it in on some paper in Ashy's room and I liked it."

Double duh.

Freight train effect going wild. Go figure. Perhaps Michael is in a position to better understand the motives of divine forces from the realm he currently occupies...

Hmm.

Besides yin, yang and all matters strange, whatever that

X factor quality is, Michael Hutchence had it nailed, and it wasn't because of the way he looked either. It was much, much more than that.

I was fortunate enough to have met Michael after attending one of his shows one night. Before that evening, I'd spent the better part of my teenage years plastering the man over my walls and collecting every piece of media I could get my hands on to add to a chunky scrapbook I'd lovingly created.

Sigh.

Yes, I was the hardcore fan, following him to every event I could, and cursing every woman he dated, Helena Christensen being the exception (Sorry Kylie!). During those hardcore years, I'd even managed a few phone conversations with him along the way.

But when the universe had finally decided it was time for our paths to collide in person, I was past the buckle-at-the-knees fangirl phase and had matured into a young woman who didn't blink twice when brushing shoulders with celebrities (Clears throat and keeps writing). Or so I had thought. In my defence, the thoughts were valid because I wasn't a stranger to spotting the odd celeb partying the night away in some VIP area of an Oxford Street Sydney club.

To make a short story even shorter, I completely caved when the moment of truth arrived and I was confronted by him. I could barely manage an audible hello much less answer his questions with anything remotely intelligent. Yep, I was suddenly drowning in a bad case of "fangirl fanatic", and totally tongue-tied.

Erm. Awkward.

That's a kind way of expressing those moments, but I do commend Michael for his efforts in lingering around, watching me with amusement and trying to engage me in some kind of rational conversation. It was just an epic fail, is all. The fact that he was trailed closely by a group of protective women frowning my way didn't help the situation either. If looks could kill, I feel sure I wouldn't have survived that night.

In any case, he was soon piled into the back of a minivan and whisked away with said women in tow, a victorious smile playing on each of their lips as they sashayed into the van after him. Eye roll. Heart plummet. I followed with a barrage of four-letter words as I watched the love of my teenage life slip into the night and vanish without so much as an autograph to my name.

Ah, the things we do. Or not do.

Michael Hutchence was a piece of gold. I learned he was special because although he possessed the above-mentioned rock star qualities, he was also very authentic. There were no airs and graces about him when he was faced with "fangirl fail" me, no traces of arrogance to his nature. In fact, every interaction I'd experienced with him was easy and real – even when I fell short in his presence. That's what made this man so unique.

I'll always be grateful for the major part Michael played during my teenage years. He and his band, INXS, provided the backdrop to many adventures, fuzzy fantasies and beautiful moments with treasured friends. I'd listen to him when the world fell from beneath my feet. I'd plug him in my Walkman and sing with him at the beach. He was there when I danced like crazy, and there during the awakening of love in my life. He was so much more than a rock star. He was a way of life, and he was some kind of special.

I write most of this post today, on January 22, 2019, on what would have been Michael's fifty-ninth birthday. I'd always taken comfort knowing he was out there, walking the earth and doing his thing. Somehow, I'd formed an invisible connection with him that I'd cherished – along with thousands of other women. It was a sad day when the world lost him. My heart ached and I cried. He was the kind of man that isn't easily forgotten. He was the kind that come here to make a difference in the world. Just listen to some of his lyrics and you'll understand what I mean.

Every now and then, I still miss him. I find the times when I'm falling short, and feeling low are the moments I reach for my earbuds, switch on one of his songs, and submerge myself in his voice. It's almost twenty-two years after his death and he still has the ability to comfort me.

Michael Hutchence was more than "Just a Man", he was revolutionary, and the world could use more like him.

Life is fleeting and precious. "Fangirl" nerves need to be conquered while you're still around to charge into the future and make every moment worthwhile. Embrace your inner rock god and walk the earth with love while you can, and while you're at it you'd do well to remember that life is not complete without seeing *Dogs in Space*.

Sigh.

As cliché as it sounds, don't wait for tomorrow to reach for the stuff that lights you up on the inside, because tomorrow may be too late.

Do you have any memorable celebrity encounters or weird signs from the universe you'd like to share with me?

KARMIC DAD

"Then what is the truth about hate? The truth about hate is love. Hate is simply love turned upside down."
~ U.S Andersen.

I was sixteen years old when I met the man who would become my stepfather. If there was ever a karmic relationship, this was it. It was a summer afternoon and he lazed across his sofa with a beer firmly nestled between his fingers. He was friendly in a stern kind of way, and he called me "Mortica" (which would fast become my nickname widely used among my friends – Mort, to be exact).

He then asked me rather bluntly if I could actually talk. I smiled and chirped back like the little shy bird I was back then, while my insides whirled at the prospect of such a loud adult confronting me about my lack of confidence.

He was my boyfriend's father.

I had no idea what to make of the man we called John, aka U.J. He was bold and indiscreet, confident and outgoing. He was larger than life, and he was everything I was not. I was very self-conscious every time I was in his company during those early days.

His extroverted nature seemed to evoke my deepest insecurities. Until I finally became comfortable around him. Of course, I had no idea at the time of the intense feelings and major role this man would eventually evoke and play in my life.

It's weird how some people stick around and can drive you insane. You see, it wasn't long after I'd met John that he in turn met my mother. It was love at first sight, and before anyone could say "what the hell is happening here?", the two of them took off on an adventure that would last almost thirty years.

Meh. There was a lot of bullshit that went along with that ride. I was young and I'd lost a mother. Naturally, I blamed John. Yes, I was surrounded by some questionable influences at the time – all with their own agenda at play. But at the end of the day, I can honestly say that it was John that had first stirred the deep feelings of hate in my belly.

I say this without an inkling of those feelings present,

and I say this with as much love as I now feel for the same person that had managed to provoke in me a hostility that I didn't quite understand.

Enter karmic relationship.

The thing was, even long after my relationship with my boyfriend had ended when I was twenty-one, I still couldn't shake John from my life.

He was there like a chunk of pasta baked to the bottom of a pan – relentless and stubborn, and no matter how hard I scrubbed, I just couldn't move that damned piece of pasta.

What do you do, right?

Choices. In the end it always comes down to choices. What we choose for ourselves is neither wrong nor right, but every time you get to choose is another chance at choosing love.

I chose love, and I chose forgiveness.

My mother had vanished from my life for seven years. That was her choice, and one I know she struggled with for a long time. I had missed her so much, more than ever when I began a family of my own.

Yet still, I remained a silent daughter in the face of her attempts to contact me. That was my choice, until I could take no more.

I could have chosen to continue to withhold her from my life and the life of her grandchildren. I could have held that sword of damnation over her head for walking out on me and my brother when I was teenager.

I could have nurtured the animosity, succumbed to the feelings of abandonment that had plagued me, and continued to punish them.

But at what cost?

I'd realised holding onto the pain and continuing to blame others for the hurt I was feeling wouldn't benefit me in any way. All it did was foster the negative feelings of depression, resentment and torment. By holding the sword of damnation over their heads, I was really balancing the blade over my own. I was punishing myself.

I was twenty-three when I next saw my mother, not long after I'd given birth to my first child, a son. He had arrived to remind me what love was really all about. He came on the breath of angels, filling the void in my heart that I hadn't known was empty, and oh, how I wanted him.

He saved me in more ways than he'll ever know, and would later reveal himself as another karmic relationship! That boy had a plan for the both of us.

The point is, the arrival of my son had reminded me that love is nothing if not forgiveness, and that people can only do the best they know how.

We all make mistakes. That's why we're here – to screw up and learn, and screw up all over again. So, I pushed aside the past and allowed it to become just that, and I slowly embarked on nurturing the relationship with my mother and stepfather again.

It wasn't always easy, and John still had the uncanny ability to drive me crazy at times. He knew how to push my buttons and sometimes found great pleasure in provoking a reaction out of me. I'd rise up and bite, and he'd respond with a chuckle, then I'd become frustrated and stalk away. We didn't always see eye to eye.

He had trouble grasping my way of thinking and my spirituality, often treating me to a "woo-woo" spooky comment of some sort. And I'd get up him for never learning how to cook a decent meal or how to wash his clothes. Oh, and when the subject of equality between the sexes arose – watch out! He'd hit a home run every time. What? It's a touchy subject with women.

Did I mention he drove me insane?

Yet, as time passed and we both matured, I learned to understand him. I learned he could only view the world from a lens in which he chose to see, or could only see, and I accepted him for everything he was, everything he tried to be, and everything he wasn't. In turn, he eventually went easy on my personal beliefs and even managed to come to respect me for it. Acceptance all around.

But the best thing about the relationship I'd experienced with my stepfather was the love born from turbulence that grew between us over thirty years. He was there when my world blackened and spun out of control.

He was there when I needed a father to talk to – his patience for listening to my dribble turned out to be darned remarkable. He was around when I just needed a good laugh, too. We shared a similar dark oddball sense of humour.

We found a common ground that connected us, and formed a bond so deep that it was me he asked for when he needed to tell someone he was dying. Someone that could talk to him about the other side.

That man that had scared the bejesus out of me when I was sixteen, had turned out to be someone I loved. He had touched my life and enriched my personal growth in ways I will never forget. He had made the effort to work through the past and listen to my shit because he loved my mother to pieces, and he loved me.

At the that time of writing this, a year has passed since his death. I miss him every day, and every day I feel his gentle touch on the side of my cheek, letting me know he's still around when I need him the most.

When times get tough and I'm batting some internal demon, I feel him stronger. I open the door and he is there. He's always there ... and I know now that he doesn't think I was as crazy as he thought when he was dwelling in his physical body.

Most of all, though, I am grateful that I chose love and forgiveness. Imagine what I would have missed out on had I chosen to stay stubborn and indifferent towards my folks?

I would have missed out on one of the most challenging and treasurable relationships of my life.

Life is made up of choices. I choose love every time. Even when I'm hurting so bad that I feel like my heart might collapse from the pain, still, I choose to qualify those emotions with love. And my life has been richer because of it.

WHO NEEDS PEOPLE? YOU DO.

*P*eople. Unless you've shunned society altogether and have carved out a piece of land for yourself someplace at the end of the earth, you cannot escape them. If, for one hypothetical moment, we agree to engage in the notion of a solitary existence, the likelihood of avoiding human beings altogether during your self-imposed isolation is still quite improbable. Let's face it, most of us will not be the outlier who chooses to embrace a Bear Grylls persona and charge off into the wilderness to live indefinitely in a log cabin in the woods.

It's a fact that people *need* other people. It's also fair to say that without interacting and forming relationships with other humans, our own abilities to love and evolve, and develop interpersonal skills such as empathy and compassion would eventually stifle before heading on a downward spiral toward emotional immaturity. You see, relationships are vital to personal, spiritual and emotional growth, and critical in fueling the embers of love from which we are born; the same realm which we will someday return.

People do need other people. Solitary confinement has been used as a form of punishment within our prison systems for hundreds of years. Isolating and stripping a human being from contact with others has a profound psychological effect. Despite its "time to reflect and connect to God" origins, there is no evidence to suggest any positive effects on inmates from time spent in solitude. In fact, the opposite is true. Solitary confinement has received severe criticism for having "detrimental psychological effects, causing trauma and an array of mental disorders, and in some cases, constituting torture".

So, for the one who concludes his existence rests on the provision of food, water and shelter and proclaims love is not vital for life and survival, I respectfully disagree. *All the food and water in the world cannot fill you enough to nourish your soul or cultivate your heart.* You might eat and drink, and you might find warmth beneath shelter, but if you are starved of the one true thing your heart and soul crave in order to grow and thrive, eventually you'll start talking to coconuts while you shrivel from the inside out and lose your mind.

The world is full of people. They are here, and they

are there. Some are good, and others are not. We need each other, *but do I need you?*

People cross our paths all the time, whether it be through social meetings and mutual acquaintances, work opportunities, meeting someone by chance at an event or some other scenario. They come and go, and for the most part they drift into the background of your past and barely summon enough effort to be thought of again.

So, how is it that we know when someone is a keeper? How do we push past the screen and the superficial courtesies that often accompany our encounters long enough to know when a connection feels right? And when do we allow our precious hearts to become vulnerable?

In 2008 I met a man during a night out with my friends at a local bar. We'd gone out to watch a band and celebrate my divorce – yes, it was an essential moment etched along the string of my life-path and warranted the celebratory occasion. I called the evening "the D-party"; I know, it's not so creative, but then again, the "D" didn't necessarily stand for divorce.

A bunch of my friends, my brother and I pulled on some threads and hit the small town of Springwood to welcome in my new life of freedom. New beginnings. I remember the evening well because it was early-July, the mountain night air was icy cold, and well, it was a great night. It wasn't often that my brother would drag himself up those mountains from Sydney to come see me, and I was delighted to spend some time with him.

It was great – the conversations were awesome, the drinks flowed and the cover band played the usual rock classics. We danced and laughed; the "D-party" was getting down and rocking it. I was totally in the moment, enjoying myself and sitting at a table with my friends when suddenly my attention was drawn to him. Like a beautiful, buff blonde vision, Mr Confident emerged from the parting crowd with me firmly in his blue-jeweled sight.

You know how it goes; heart temporarily seizes, pulse ramps up a notch and all of a sudden, you're feeling a little more than heady. I mean this guy was close to perfect. So perfect, I almost felt pale in comparison. When his lips spread into a wide grin and he greeted me as he took the chair beside me, it took all I had not to focus on the dropping jaws of my girlfriends as they ogled him.

As it turned out, he was an athlete and had mutual acquaintances with my friend's husband in the professional sporting arena. He was friendly and charming; charisma oozed from each deliberate remark and gesture as he set about making me the center of his universe. And when he realized the big guy in the corner chair was my brother, he put out all the stops to impress.

Mr nice-guy. Mr cool-cat. Mr can-I-take-you-out-for-dinner-next-week-when-you're-all-alone-guy.

Of course, I agreed. Why wouldn't I? It was a no-brainer. The man was hot, and I was available. There were no rings on my fingers, and I thought it might be about time to dip my toes into the perilous depths of the dating game. My friends thought he was awesome, and my brother gave his nod of approval too. I had nothing to lose.

Or so I thought.

There's that thing about me, the part that believes the good in everyone and takes people at face value. I assume the best in people's intentions. I never intentionally set out to hurt people, so *why* would they want to hurt me?

In hindsight, the signs were there. Had I paid closer attention to a few of his mannerisms the night I met him, I might have avoided the date night. Had I listened to the way my incessant nerves tortured me right up till the moment he knocked on my door to take me out, I might have avoided him forcing himself on me. I might have avoided the breach of my personal safety and the ordeal of being violated, but I didn't.

It's not that I dislike sex. On the contrary, I'm quite partial to the steamy activity. No other act can fuse two people together so deeply, so intimately. When two people are in love their connection and hunger for each other expands, flows and thrives as they merge themselves completely through love-making. *This is fusion in all its wonderous glory; physically, mentally, soulfully.* It is the kind of stuff we live for and crave above all else; the ultimate expression of love that transports us to higher realms. *Exquisite realms.*

Of course, not all sex is like that. Sometimes, we just need to be close to another human. Sometimes, we just want to have fun. All good, as long we all understand each other.

I saw a man once. I met him during a trip to Canada. He was seven years younger than me, eager as a bucking bull on rodeo night, and packed just like one, if you know what I mean. He boarded a plane and travelled to Australia to spend some quality time with me. Twice. He happened to arrive in my life when it was exactly the kind of quality time I was looking for. Right on time. I did things with that guy I hadn't ever done before. Or since. We understood each other.

Until his possessive tendencies kicked in and he didn't want to leave.

The point is, mutually agreed upon sex is an awesome part of being human. I enjoy sex. More than likely, you do too. But if I'm *not* feeling it, then I'm not feeling it and it's not on – period.

Mr Horny-cool-cat had other ideas.

There's that the thing about some people – you know, the ones that have trouble understanding *that* part about sex. They are the same kind of people that play games and reel you in, the ones that get off on power tripping and saying the right things at the right times to gain the trust they don't deserve. They show you what they want you to see in order to get what they want from you. Those kinds of people are dangerous because their truth is probably false, even to themselves.

Want to hear the real kicker? He called me the following week to ask me out on another date. When I ignored his calls, he pinged me with a text. I mean, really? I'm not sure if he was clueless or cunning as a rat's ass. Either way, seeing his number appear on my phone sparked the anxiety attack that had landed me in the emergency room the day following our first date.

We can never really know what lies beneath the exterior that a person chooses to present to the world. Hell, even Mr Gorgeous had my usually doubtful brother fooled – and that's saying something. Not to mention my over-protective friends. It was the clean-cut, white-toothed, good-guy image he had going for him, and it worked a treat. I can only imagine how many victims he has tallied up on his date-rape quest, and I can only hope that he eventually encountered more than he bargained for.

I know that Mr Confident became my experience because he was the final thread that released me from men like him infecting my life. He was the catalyst in reminding me what I didn't want and what I refused to settle for – *bullies and men who didn't respect women*. In the end, though, without taking the time to look beyond our initial encounters and getting to know someone who captures our attention, how would we know the keepers from the rubble? How would we harness and nurture the important connections destined to cross our paths?

We wouldn't. Yet, I know now to pay more attention to my internal warning system and give it the trust it deserves. People *need* other people. Sometimes, we do have to take a chance and put ourselves out there, because if we don't, we might end up talking to coconuts and dancing naked with a broomstick to Prince's *Let's Go Crazy*. Or worse, ***we might miss the greatest love of our lives***.

I've learned by honoring and loving myself first, that I will attract those with the best intentions in all arenas of my life. They are the diamonds in the rough; those special ones that are sent here to shine over you and touch your life in a magical way. You can't miss them – they are the ones that make the little moments special; the ones unafraid to love.

Treasure your diamonds for not only are they rare, they form the groundwork beating your heart with love.

ROOMS FOR THE MEMORY – WHAT'S IT REALLY ABOUT ANYWAY?

I will never forget the final months of my stepfather's life, nor the day I got the call summoning my presence because there was something urgent that he and my mother needed to tell me. I didn't hesitate that day. Instead, I blew off the words of the project I'd been working on and drove the short distance to my folk's place who live in the next town. All the while, my stomach churned and my nerves fluttered. Somehow, I knew before I arrived that it was cancer.

We hear about it all the time, people dying of cancer. In Australia, cancer is the leading cause of death. Still, nothing can prepare you when it reaches so close to home. I had lost a beloved uncle to cancer years before, but I wasn't around to witness those horrendous end days. I got the call to come and say goodbye that final day, but by the time I had arrived at the hospital he was gone. I'd missed him by fifteen minutes and it tore me apart on the inside.

It was different with my dad. I was closer to him and it was me that he sought when he wanted to talk about death. For all the beliefs and spiritual teachings I had devoured and practiced over the years, I found myself struggling for the right words to say to him. What do you say when someone you love is dying? What words can you offer without sounding like a Tao scroll banner?

What did I really know about death anyway?

My mother is the eternal optimist. She couldn't or wouldn't allow herself to accept that he was dying – right up until the day I told her that it was time to call my sister, my aunt and cousin to say their goodbyes. I remember the expression on her face when she heard me say those words; the shock as realization dawned. In those moments, the tables had turned; I had become her rock and her carer. There was no return. The fight was almost over, and I knew she had one foot in reality and the other in disbelief.

It was Friday afternoon, he was incoherent, dazed, and he couldn't walk unassisted. Their home had been transformed into something that resembled a medical centre. He hadn't wanted to spend his last days in a hospital, palliative care turned up every few hours to administer morphine and check in on him and my mother.

By that time, there were no more words to tell him

except ones of love and surrender. Those last hours were like a living nightmare. Nobody tells you what its like at the end of a cancer battle. Nobody tells you how watching someone you love writhe and grasp onto the final threads of life kills you on the inside. Stubborn man. Right up till the end, and it was his love for my mother that kept him hanging on. He'd been so worried about her life after his death that he tried so hard to stay for her. For her. Even though he was no longer afraid of death.

I'd whispered in his ear and told him that she would be okay, that we would all look after her, that it was okay for him leave now. We all told him.

From Friday afternoon, he fought as hard as I'd ever seen anyone fight. He fought for love. I couldn't stay with him and my mother the entire time, but my sister and her husband did. I tag-teamed with my husband because we have young children, but even from my home a few miles away, his presence was all around me.

February 18th, 2018 was a beautiful summer Sunday morning. I'd been with them till late the night before, and my husband wanted to be there too. So, I turned to my writing to fill in my mind as I impatiently waited for him to return so I could get over there. I was working *Rebellion* when the call came. He'd gone without me. He wasn't supposed to leave without me there. But he did, and I didn't get to hear him take another breath, or whisper in his ear one last time.

He left and the day was gloriously blue and hollow.

He left and my life has never been the same. It's when the profound moments arrive that we realise life stops for nothing and no one. The same moments when we know our human mortality in its truest form and acknowledge how fleeting our life on this earth really is, and how final death seems when you can no longer pick up the phone and call your dad.

My mother had wanted to dress him before the funeral. She wanted nobody else but me to accompany her. I watched as she shaved him, spoke softly to him while stroking his face and kissing him as she placed his favourite beanie on his head and fixed his shirt. I stood in the corner of the room fidgeting and feeling numb. He didn't seem real to me anymore – he was empty and frozen, and he was just gone. I couldn't relate to him in that way because it was no longer him.

I'd felt the distinct difference of his soul no longer occupying his body. His body was just that; a soulless carcass that no longer represented my father. I knew I could get closer to him in other ways because I felt him all around us. Those feelings made me feel awkward during the dressing, I was relieved when it was over and I couldn't get out of there quick enough.

A few years ago, my step-father and mother stayed with us for a few days. Those were the days when they'd lived interstate and travelled around Australia a lot of the time. One evening, we sat beneath the stars after dinner and chatted over a few drinks and music. That night he'd told me that a day will come in the future when he was dead and gone, that I would remember that night with fond memories and a smile. That I would think of the wise words he so readily bestowed on me and remember him.

We didn't always see things the same way. We disagreed quite often. He was a fatherless man that strived and struggled to provide the guidance of a father, and he was interested in my work and life as a writer. He'd written and published a book himself. Watching me do my writing thing made him proud.

Although I'd pushed his words aside that night, it turns out that he was right – I do recall that night with a smile in my heart, and not because of the guidance he tried to provide, but because of the love he had always shown me.

I have realized that even in death, he has continued to teach me. Nothing ever before has had such an impact on my life. In death, he has taught me that love *is* eternal; that it really does transcend time and space, and that the way we love in this lifetime matters.

There are a few people in this world who I love but are not currently in my life. People that I have shared time with, loved from the moment we met and haven't stopped loving them since. If this is it – if this all I have to let them know that I still care, then every one of these words matters as much as the love that exists within me. If this moment is all we have, I'll bubble it with precious love and hope they receive it because the way we love matters. And whether those people realize it or not, my love matters too.

THE GIRL CAN SHINE

"Everything you want is on the other side of fear." – Jack Canfield

I used to be afraid of so many things. When I was a child, I was scared of growing up and facing a life without my parents. I was afraid of the Easter Bunny and the milkman, and the thought of death had my head spinning in a thousand directions. Most of all, I was afraid of being myself. I never knew who I really was beneath the fleshy exterior and the questionable outfits my mother dressed me in. I was super self-conscious, and I couldn't quite figure out my place in the world. The only place I felt comfortable was in the inner sanctuary of my mind.

Insecurity is a strange thing to ponder. Where does it spring from? How does it cultivate and flourish even under pleasant living conditions? My early childhood home was a safe and loving environment. Both of my parents are wonderful people, and my mother worked on strengthening my self-perception. Yet, no matter what she did or said, there was a constant underlying feeling of inadequacy shadowing my every waking moment. I felt awkward and self-conscious almost all the time – to the point that I was crippled on the inside. I had allowed those self-deprecating emotions to squander many opportunities throughout my early adulthood, which played a massive role in accepting the mistreatment of others.

I was around six years old when my parents took me and my little brother one weekend to visit family friends who lived in Sydney's north shores. If you're familiar with Sydney, you'll know those beautiful northern beaches and suburbs are populated with the spectacular homes reserved for the wealthy and famous. As it happened, one of my mother's girlfriends had recently married a lovely man with readymade kids, a seriously humongous mansion on the north shore, and a rather well-oiled, erratic mental disorder – and we, the nuclear family from the southern burbs, were lugging up for a weekend to experience how the other half lived.

I must be honest here, I was pumped. I mean, the moment I laid eyes on that outrageously big home, my breath caught somewhere in my lungs and my heart thundered in wonder. I know when you're that age everything seems bigger than what it really is, but I can tell you that that home was set back among lofty trees and overlooked a lush valley leading to the water, and it was the most beautiful home I'd ever seen.

The interior of the manor was four levels of wonderment. The plush piled rooms were spacious, the kitchen and bathrooms were shiny and modern, and the Barbie-lookalike girl of the house slept beneath an elaborate weave of lace on the biggest bed I'd ever seen. Well, for a child's standards anyhow.

She looked like a character straight out of one of my Golden Books, and even had a romantic name – Krystal – and I swear, when she clasped her delicate fingers around mine and rushed me toward her bedroom, I froze at the threshold and blinked – had I suddenly been pulled through a rabbit hole and emerged between the pages of a Golden Book?

As I gazed around the candy-colored room brimming with the latest gadgets, a huge doll house and all the toys under the rainbow, I decided I had. I wasn't aware that other little girls slept beneath draping sheer fabric other than in the movies and my books. I had to be in a fairytale – there was no other explanation.

Considering that up until that moment I had shared a rather small room with my little brother, you can understand how that possibility was a viable option for me.

After I managed to pull myself from the initial reaction to Krystal's room, I allowed her to entice me further into her lair. She was excited to show me all her wonderful things, and I was eager to see them. Yet as she moved around the vast pink room with her chest puffed, her golden hair flowing down her back and her baby blues peering from a china-doll face, something else began to happen – me.

This stunning little creature with cherry-colored rosettes for lips and the glossiest blonde hair I'd seen outside of my Barbie doll collection had me enthralled. The thick carpet beneath my feet seemed to suck me further into its twisted pile and my entire body shifted into something extremely awkward as it dawned on me that this *was* a fairy tale and *she* was a real-life princess.

So, what did that make me?

Erm. Well, I'm going with the ugly duckling analogy here because that's exactly how I felt. Better that than the wicked stepmother.

This lovely princess was confident and pretty, and she didn't seem to second guess herself. She didn't have to as this was a girl who appeared to have it all. She glided around the carpet like a swan skimming the calm blue ocean, gracefully flicking her hair when she laughed. And she laughed a lot. Turned out, she was a killer on the dance floor too – I know this because our parents took us out for dinner to a club that had a dance competition on the Saturday night and forced us kids to get on stage and boogie.

She won, by the way. Surprise, surprise.

The point is that this china-doll was everything I was not. She was perfect. I spent most of the weekend shrinking on the inside while my insecurities burned like a wildfire. If I could tell my younger self anything, I would remind her to love herself just a bit more than what she did, and I would tell her not to be afraid to shine. Because, at the end the day, that's what insecurities boil down to – lack of self-love and self-belief.

I keep banners around my house. These are wonderful wise snippets shared from the likes of native American beliefs and other ancient spiritual teachings. They're everywhere. They're in the kitchen, my office, the loo, my bedroom ... I even have one hanging in my closet. I am someone that needs to constantly remind myself of the bigger picture, as I can become overwhelmed with life at times, and I know how easy it can be to slip back into old thinking patterns – those childhood feelings of inadequacy are never really that far below the surface.

One of my favorites is from Nelson Mandela when he talks about fear. Part of the quote is as follows:

"It is our light not our darkness, that most frightens us.

We ask ourselves, who am I to be brilliant, gorgeous, talented, fabulous?

Actually, who are we not to be?"

I love these words, and I realize now that playing small doesn't serve the world, and that shrinking into the darkness and dimming *my* light doesn't benefit me and won't enrich *my* life. I won't grow and flourish by continuing to doubt myself and think small.

I have come a long way since that little "ugly duckling" plagued with insecurities, and it didn't come easy to reach the point where I am now. I had to deliberately set out to adjust my inner-perspectives and practice a bucket load of intentional change in my thought patterns, but over the years I've been able to tame the self-doubts and insecurities to something manageable.

Do I always get it right? Nope. But each time I feel that wobble, the one that says, "Who do you think you are to be doing what you're doing?", I take a few breaths and remind myself that *a life lived in fear is a life half lived*, and then I keep going, pushing myself to take the chances; putting myself out there in ways I could never have imagined, telling people how I really feel and baring my soul to the world. I do this because I am here to experience, expand, evolve and love like crazy. Why hold back when time is not on your side?

So, the next time you feel that fear-wobble circling down your spine and threatening to overcome you, remember that everything you want is on the other side of fear, and consider these words from Nelson Mandela: *"As we let our own light shine, we unconsciously give other people permission to do the same. As we are liberated from our own fear, our presence automatically liberates others."*

You too are a magnificent swan – and the ocean is your playground. Come fly with me.

SCANDALOUS: A FLEETING LOVE SONG

*D*o you remember your first broken heart?

You do, right?

I'm not talking about the crush you had on that cute guy or girl during middle school that resulted in a wounded heart for a day or two.

I'm talking about the first time you felt as if your heart had split in two and spilled with the blood of utter misery. The time you cried yourself to sleep every night and awoke with the weight of the world on your shoulders.

You know what I'm talking about.

It was the same time when every love song you'd ever known suddenly resonated. No longer was *Islands in the Stream* just a chirpy tune you knew off by heart. *That music. Those words.* They weren't just catchy vibes you sang along with to the radio anymore.

Uh-uh. No sirree. Your world had spun off its axis and nothing would ever be the same again. You had leveled up to a different ball game and you'd just lost the first innings.

Welcome to heartbreak central.

Don't forget to grab your tissues at the door while you drown yourself in the music that now transcended into something meaningful. Something solemnly expressive. Something ... raw. Lyrics. Tunes. Voices. Instruments. All of them pulsed, beaten and drummed against your brain like a weeping melody that etched a memorable notch on your freshly bruised heart.

I Wish it Would Rain Down on Me – Phil Collins.

"Cos, I know in my heart of hearts I'm never gonna hold you again" – I mean, come on. I almost broke the cassette tape hitting the rewind button. I choked. The stereo choked. But I did it – I abused that rewind button till the surface was worn smooth while I sprawled on my bed and gazed teary eyed at the ceiling wondering how he could have rejected me.

How?

Love Song – Prince and Madonna.

A love song with swag ... Attitude ... Sass.

"Say what you mean, mean what you say. This is *not* a love song."

"I'm losing my mind (are you wasting my time)."

Gaslighting?

Hmm. Another subject.

He was my friend's older brother and he liked Prince. He drove his parents' car and he played the *Batman* soundtrack every time I rode with him.

Scandalous – Prince.

"*Understand, understand that I love you.*"

Baby.

He could dance. Oh, how he could dance. He had the moves and the grind. His hair would fall over his brow as he worked his hips and did sexy things with his lips. He asked me to dance at the high school disco, and holy mother of all things hot, I had never been so turned on.

Mind you, I was only sixteen. And sweet.

Didn't matter how sweet I was, by the following day, word had spread around like a blazing wildfire – He and Kim looked as if they needed a bed last night.

Erm... huh? Nah.

He must have heard it through the *Grapevine*, because it didn't take long for my home phone to ring. Remember how phones used to be attached to the wall socket in a common area in your home and the curly cord could only reach so far?

Ours was in a small hallway leading to the bedrooms and the bathroom, smack bang in the midst of a heavy traffic zone. No matter how hard I tried, I couldn't stretch that damned cord far enough to reach my room. I tried hard.

Sweet talker crooned down the line. He's all smooth.

"Hi baby."

Blushing. He called me, baby?

I'm suddenly feeling rather mature .

"Hi," I said, gushing.

"I had fun last night."

Blushing plus heart flip.

Definitely feeling all-woman now.

"Me too."

"Can I take you out on a date this Saturday night?"

Blushing plus heart flip plus inner-delighted scream.

Slight alarmed pause, then: "Hold on, I'll just ask my mum."

The grown-up feelings fizzled fast after that, especially when she slapped me with a strict curfew of 10pm.

Wait – what? *10pm?*

I know, right? I debated. Hell, I argued till I was blue in the face. I was good at debating with my mother. I was also good at losing those battles. She was nervous. I was going out on my first date with an older boy who drove a car. What was her deal, anyway?

I didn't understand ...

He took me to Darling Harbour. He held my hand and we walked along the harborside and gazed at the city fountains cascading beneath fairy lights that sprinkled and twinkled in the trees above us. *Sigh.*

Sound romantic?

It was. To me. Those moments were the same ones that bonded us. Well, I can't speak for him, but that was my perception, *my experience*. It was short-lived though, because I had a curfew, remember, and he had other pressing matters to attend to within that timeframe.

Like, get into my pants.

"Whisper, whisper a question."

He parked at the beach and asked me to join him in the back seat of the car. He introduced me to lust and desire, and the hottest kissing session I'd ever known. He introduced me to dry-humping.

"With my body, I'll scream a reply."

The chemistry was amazing, and I was falling *in love*. Foreign things began happening to my body; my head whirled, pulse ramped, nipples ached and something else – I got wet. Really wet.

Who knew that could happen? Not me.

Temperatures rose higher than a tsunami on amphetamines. The car windows fogged. We were covered in kisses and sweat and trapped in a steamy mobile Turkish bath on high arousal. My sweater was off. Bra still intact. It was at this point he moved in for the kill – the zipper on my jeans.

Panic set in.

"Don't be afraid, baby. Touch it and explode."

It was going to explode alright. There was no mistaking

the bulge, and absolutely zero doubt that he wanted to get unzipped and release its throbbing wrath upon me. It was then I put on the brakes.

"Stop!"

"Huh?" Breath hot and urgent in my ear. Spaghetti hands in a frenzy. "No, why? We're having fun."

I couldn't argue with that, but I wasn't going to lose my virginity in the back seat of a car on a first date – no matter how much I liked him.

He didn't like that.

"Take me home."

He didn't like that either.

"Please."

Suddenly, I was silently grateful for my early curfew and had an inkling why my mother had been so nervous about this date. We rode in silence and he said he'd call me. He didn't.

Enter Phil Collins on rewind.

What is it with guys not calling you if you don't give out? Dicks.

After that, he systematically made his way through a lot of pretty girls in my year who *did* give out. I think he appreciated systems. Yes, he liked his systems.

The girls, however, did not. They put out and he called on them again – until they inevitably wound up sobbing along to Phil Collins. Or Millie Vanilli.

"I knew it from the start you would break my heart."

I might've silently smirked when watching mascara tears staining virtuous faces black as one pretty girl after the other caught the backdraft of his sting. He hurt me too, but it could have been worse; I could have been one of them black-stained notches on his belt. I could've slept with him.

He called me again a few months down the track. He was ready for round two. I guess he thought I'd matured enough to get all-woman with him.

That time, I turned down his invitation. Not saying it was easy, though.

That smile. Those deep brown eyes. Luscious lips … steamy mobile Turkish baths and hand holding in Darling Harbour beneath twinkling lights. *Sigh*.

"No thanks."

Choke. Did I just turn down the most irresistible guy in school?

Yep. He shattered my heart for crying out loud. There was no return ticket. I did the time. I cried, I wrote him letters (and actually posted one to him – cringe); I moped around for days, weeks … months.

Then I found a spot in my mind and placed him on a shelf and moved on.

Witnessing his playboy antics probably helped some too. Black tears leave lasting strong impressions.

About six months ago I heard from him again. I was

going through a tough time. My heart was hurting when he pinged me out of the blue.

It was as if the universe was reminding me of the past. It was reminding me that hearts break, and hearts heal, and everything would be alright.

Serendipity.

"I should write a book about my life. It would be a bestseller!" he told me.

"Oh, hey, I know. You can begin your book about the time you broke my heart."

"Did I really? That was never my intention."

Erm ... yeah. Duh. Did you not get that letter? (cringe). I'm certain I spoke for myself earlier about the bonding and romance part along a dark Darling Harbour street. Luminous city fountains and fairy light dreams.

Yeah.

"You have my sincerest apologies. Believe it or not I have often thought about you over the years."

Hmm. I wonder had I not put on the brakes in the steam-machine that night if that would have turned out differently.

Either way, whatever it was that we shared has made its mark against our memories and formed part of the fabric of who we both are today.

I must admit he's a pretty cool guy with a vibrant personality, though. Whenever I hear from him, he always makes me laugh. It's not unusual to receive something like this in Messenger nowadays:

"What's up, ex-girlfriend with a broken heart? HAHA!"

"Cute :)"

"Spirits rise and spirits fall."

DIRTY DANCING

"Nobody puts Baby in the corner."
- Johnny Castle

I always wondered what happened after Johnny plucked "Baby" from that corner and they were done with that last dance. Did they make it?

We got the pay-off in the form of Johnny asserting his position for his girl, experiencing the feel-good pleasures when our bad boy came back for our protagonist. Our hearts fluttered and soared as he mouthed the words "I've had the time of my life. No, I've never felt this way before" while holding her close. Yet, as the credits rolled out to the catchy tune, I found myself somewhat mystified.

Call me a stick-in-the-mud if you must, but I was never

completely sold on that romance. The chemistry between Patrick Swayze and Jennifer Grey lingered somewhere in the sludge I'm playing with, getting my hands dirty while seemingly bagging the movie.

In the context of relationships, chemistry is a simple feeling people get when they share a special connection. It's that underlying impulse and need to see the other person again, to be close to them – a romantic spark. This is the part between the characters that I felt wasn't conveyed through the screen.

Having said that, I must somewhat digress. Just a little. I'm thinking of the scene where "Baby" shows up at Johnny's doorstep after her father saved Penny from certain death following a dodgy abortion. Johnny tells her he's never met anyone like her, that she's not scared of anything. Her response gets me every time when she says:

"Me? I'm scared of everything; I'm scared of what I saw, of what I did, of who I am. Most of all I'm scared of walking out of this room and never feeling my whole life the way I feel when I'm with you."

Sigh.

That is one great dialog delivered with just the right amount of vulnerability. You can grumble all you want about not being a romantic, but if that line doesn't make you feel something, then perhaps your heart is caked with a thick slick of that mud you thought I was stuck in.

Want me to help you get clean?

The truth is, I'm not writing about *Dirty Dancing* today because I wanted to talk about romance or sexual chemistry. Despite my personal take on the on-screen chemistry (or lack thereof) between Patrick and Jennifer, the romantic "coming of age" love story hit the archetypical "forbidden love" romance conventions superbly, making a gazillion dollars worldwide and going on to become the first film to sell more than a million copies for home video.

Obviously, something worked. Maybe it was that line of Baby's. Or the undeniably hot dancing scenes, which let's face it, sizzled up movie screens and temperatures the world over. Someone pass me the ice as I gear up to tell you something strange.

Strange things. Other than people, the universe is always communicating and responding to us in some way. It may sound a touch on the "woo-woo" side and whether you believe or not is your thing. But it's when you begin to tune into yourself and the energy around you that you start to become aware of the most uncanny and wonderful things happening for you.

I hadn't thought about *Dirty Dancing* for the longest of times, yet now, it seems to have become something in my life. At least, temporarily. No, I'm not planning on taking Mambo or Salsa lessons, or writing a romance novel any time soon (I'll leave the romance writing to Catherine Evans). It's just that suddenly, this romantic 1987

American flick has begun to shadow me and I'm not entirely sure why.

It began a few weeks back when I meandered to the couch with my plate of dinner and flicked on the TV. *Dirty Dancing* flitted onto the screen. This is the only time I might actually watch something on TV, and only for the length of time it takes for me to finish eating. It was good enough to grab my attention for that snippet of time.

I felt something shift slightly within me. When you become attuned to the universal consciousness, your inner reactions to your senses are a telltale sign to pay attention. Still, I switched off the movie after about 15 minutes and thought no more of it.

Fast forward one week and I experienced a repeat. That's right. I grabbed my dinner, made for the couch, turned on the TV and there it was again, *Dirty Dancing*. This time, I'd caught the above-mentioned scene; Solomon Burke's *Cry to Me* caught somewhere in my chest as I bit my lip and turned off the TV.

Gets even stranger. I downloaded the album so I could hear that song again. Only, that track isn't included on the iTunes soundtrack (true). But, *She's Like the Wind* is, and it grabbed my attention, so I listened. When the song traveled from my buds and into my ears, what happened was something I'll never forget.

The following day, that same song was playing when I stopped by my local store to pick a few things, and ever since I downloaded the album, my iPad has taken to randomly playing *She's Like the Wind* all on its own. Which has never happened before. Like, ever.

My mother often wonders why stuff like this occurs in my life. I tell her it's not that the signs aren't there for her, but that she's not paying enough attention to catch onto them. When we make a conscious choice to become aware of and push beyond our preconceived ideas of the world, we begin to open our mind to perceive and receive more information from a greater intelligence. And I can't begin to convey the appreciation I feel to be able to tap into this part of our world.

As these beautiful unseen forces are currently slapping me in the face with a bit of the *Dirty* stuff, I can't help but wonder again what had struck me so long ago when first watching the movie. After the summer spent at the Catskills Resort and it was time to return to the "real world", did Johnny and "Baby" ever make it? Was their love strong enough to overcome the obstacles they would have had to face?

I guess we make up that part of the story as we go.

IT'S A SEX TYPE THING

When I was sixteen, I met a boy. He was a year older than me, a rev-head and kind of cute. He gave me roses and bought me things made of gold, and he was the first boy I slept with. I didn't hold out for long. Three weeks to be exact. The sex topic was hot on the agenda back then and I was eager to explore.

About a year beforehand, a girlfriend found an old book and brought it to school. I don't know where she had unearthed that book. It was a tattered paperback brimming with pornographic stories. None of us had experienced sex, but man, we couldn't get enough of that book.

We'd huddle together during the lunch break and read it aloud, our eyes popping from their sockets with tales of gigantic penises and horny women doing stuff we'd never thought possible. It sure beat the sex-ed classes dished out by our all-girl high school.

That first time is never what you expect it to be. There were no earth-shattering orgasms rocking my world. In fact, there were no orgasms during that five-year relationship – period.

I got good at faking it, though. Even thereafter, the all-important climax via penetration eluded me for years. I learned how to master the fake orgasm. Every woman probably does at some point.

Luckily, my first husband was gifted in other areas. Like cunnilingus. I thanked the heavens for that because the rev-head thought going down on a woman was like a Pacman game at an all-you-can-eat pellet buffet. Munch ... munch.

Ouch.

How is it that some guys don't understand the art of cunnilingus? I mean, we're not walking around with an impenetrable armor between our legs. There are some delicate bits going on down there. Think pressure, but soft and steady, use fingers at the same time and for god's sake, when a woman is moaning like a breathless goddess, don't stop and change tactics all of a sudden – you might just interrupt the flow. Oh yeah and keep the sharp ends of your teeth out of it and the hardcore sucking for a lollipop.

I stayed with the rev-head until I was twenty-one. During that time, my single girlfriends were living that life. You know, the one where you work all week and come the weekends, you're hitting the club scene and partying hard.

Occasionally, I'd join them. But rev-head was into clubbing and he disliked the thought of me venturing out without him. Too many fellas on the horizon, you see.

He wasn't wrong. My friends were into one-night stands for a while there. The thought intrigued me – great, casual sex with a stranger and no strings attached. Sounded like one of those Jackie Collins novels I'd readily devoured years earlier.

Those characters had the BEST sex with strangers. By the time things were over with rev-head, I was determined to fulfill the fantasy. I was going to embark on my first one-nighter.

He was a Croatian guy and a bit older than me. He took me back to his pad and introduced me to his bedroom before introducing me to the biggest penis I'd ever seen.

Of course, at the time I'd only one other to compare it to. I swear, he almost broke me with that thing. It was as thick as a tree trunk and just as hard. He was speeding too. Which meant, the end was nowhere in sight. For him. It was a different story for me, though. Round one and I was out, hobbling back home as the sun began to rise.

He called me a few days later, and a few times again after that wanting to see me. Umm... since when did a one-nighter turn into more? That rarely happened in a J.C. novel. I don't even know how he got my number. Besides, one round with what he was packing was more than enough.

Fast forward twelve years and divorced, I was ready to try another one-nighter. The driving thought was that my now husband was completely doing my head in and seemed to have difficulty deciding if he wanted me or not.

Well, let's rephrase that – he wanted me, just on his terms, and his terms meant he could come and go as he pleased ... and perhaps fuck other women in between those bouts of silence when he was "emotionally torn about what to do". Poor baby. So, I eventually decided to take a page out of his book and hook up with someone.

Small towns. Everyone knew my husband in that town. He was one of those guys – you know, the suave, confident type that had no trouble picking up women and systematically made his way through half of the town.

Of course, I had no idea of his reputation when our paths crossed. How could I? I was a single mother that rarely left the house. It was when my folks happened to be visiting from out of town and I ventured out with some friends one Saturday night that I met him. And no, I didn't go home with him that night. Although, he tried very hard to persuade me otherwise.

The point is, when I went out with the intention to hook up with someone, I ended up with a sweet man that knew my beau. Yeah. He had a friend too. No, I'm not about to tell you I had a threesome. His friend was a fireman and hooked up with my girlfriend.

Those two didn't waste any time. They made for the

bedroom as soon as we arrived at their place, leaving me with my guy and a whole bunch of *"what the hell am I doing here?"* thoughts racing through my head.

He didn't push it, so we hung out and talked for a while before eventually fooling around a bit. That's when it got awkward. The moment he entered me I started to cry. *Say what?* I know, right. Things didn't stay too hard after that. The fire had fizzled beneath my steady stream of tears. I can't imagine how he felt, other than it being an epic fail. I guess I'm not cut out to be a J.C. character after all.

End of one-nighters for me.

So, I pull on my clothes with thoughts of wanting to get the fuck out of that house as soon as possible. I barge into the bedroom where my girlfriend was sprawled on the bed – legs wide, fireman bottom up, face buried deep between her thighs. Remember what I said about not stopping when you're on the magic roll in the cunnilingus department?

My girlfriend wanted to kill me. Still, I'd interrupted their moment and despite her efforts to usher me away, I wasn't budging. She had the car, I needed to leave. We left. But not before she demanded that he call her. He didn't.

I ran into that sweet guy a couple of months later and he gave me a big hug. I was out with my husband. By that time, he'd come to his senses and realized that a love like that doesn't show up every so often, and that sex with someone you love is SO much better than the fleeting exchanges between strangers.

And finally, after years of wondering if it was possible, I'd discovered that earth-shattering orgasms can be achieved through penetration. And it blew my mind, among other things.

LOVE ON A TRAIN

"Wouldn't you rather have a deep, passionate relationship than something that feels more like friendship? Life is too short to live a single moment without passion – especially in your relationship."
- Tony Robbins

The Ancient Greeks called it *Ludus* – the feeling of infatuation in the early days of romance. Ah, those sweet moments when your stomach flutters at the sight of new love and every second spent apart feels like internal torture. Falling in love is one of life's greatest pleasures. After all, it is love that forms the basis of our humanity and influences our lives from the moment we are born. But hands down, the best part of those first stages in a relationship has to be the lust that accompanies our every waking hour.

Like most of us, those curious Ancient Greeks were smitten by love. Their fascination in the devotion department motivated them enough to spent time studying love in all its forms. The Greek God of fertility proved to be the inspiration behind what the Ancient Greeks called *Eros* - the realm of love encompassing desire, fire and passion.

Now we're getting somewhere.

Long days filled with intense yearning between bouts of time spent ensnared in erotic flashes of the night before – daydreams of the moments when a thin layer of sweat was all that separated you and your lover. You know what I'm talking about it. Those sensually shaded days where you exist in a constant state of arousal. He is all you can think about; all you want to think about.

A deep need to release sexual energy becomes your driving thought while your panties are constantly suffering beneath the heat. You're certain that you've stepped straight out of a scene from Basic Instinct. Minus the ice pick.

Wait – keep the ice pick. You're going to need it.

Burn, baby, burn.

That statement can be considered somewhat tame when my second husband swept into my life to change everything I thought I knew about passion. Late nights involving lips and tongues, black lace, delicious fingers ... rock hard parts between hot wet places.

Lovers whisper secrets only they two can hear. Bodies entangle to become a river; hips move faster than a runaway train. Nothing is forbidden. Long held fantasies become your reality.

The sexual tension between us was intoxicating; hot and consuming. So much so, seldom could we refrain from keeping our hands off each when out in public. We used to fuck everywhere – the dark corners in a club; the lady's bathroom; shopfront doorways; shady parks; cars. We even did it on the neighbor's front porch. What? I hear you cry. She was the neighbor from hell. This was our payback. Heh.

When you are in the throes of a hedonistic realm where the pursuit of sexual pleasure becomes your primary focus, nothing is taboo. Nothing is off limits. Love doesn't know limits or boundaries. Love only knows expression.

Ever since *Risky Business* had erupted onto my screen, I had wanted to fuck on a train. You remember the scene - hot passionate kisses; locked eyes while having sensual sex in a dimly lit and empty carriage on a fast-moving train.

Exciting. Steamy. Carnal.

Anyone want to take a train ride? After that scene, I am certain trains across the world knew more than just the average commuter. Perhaps this was the driving force behind the exercise to install security cameras on every carriage. Who needs to watch choreographed porn when you can get the real-life stuff on late night train rides?

Psyche.

It was on. The evening arrived and one the most erotic acts I have ever experienced preceded the train sex, becoming part of a long-winded evening of foreplay. We were out in a crowded bar listening to a band and enjoying a few drinks. Knee-high boots worn with sheer panty-hose beneath a short skirt doesn't make for easy access when in public.

So, he held my eyes with his own and slipped his hand between my thighs, lightly rubbing me with the back of his fingers before he pulled away and brought his fingers beneath his nose, inhaling my scent. Body heat. Groan. My sexual hormones went into overdrive watching that simple act play out. I think I blushed beneath the immediate rush of arousal. Someone flag a train; I was in need. Desperate need.

The carriage wasn't as nearly as dark or as empty as the *Risky Business* train scene, but business went ahead regardless. How could it not after the abovementioned prologue?

It was bright, starkly bright and it didn't take long to figure out we had to maneuver our way around those sheer panty hose tucked within a high pair of leathers.

He got creative; slipping my panties and hose down

until they bunched at the top of my boots before dropping to his knees and crawling up between my legs. He was essentially ensnared between boots, hose and thighs with no way out but onward. Some might call that a pussy-trap. He would probably agree. Either way, he was hard and I was ready, and he proceeded to bang the shit out of me while the train sped west and a few folks lingered in the back of the carriage pretending not to notice.

Risky Business eat your heart out. Not really. I mean, it was seriously hot, but somehow, we didn't manage to reach that slowed-down climatic filming achieved in the movie. I didn't feel like Rebecca De Mornay – despite the security cameras rolling overhead and particularly when it was over and I came back up for air, spotting cheesy grins flashing from the back of the carriage.

Blush.

The Ancient Greeks didn't necessarily think that *Eros* was always a good thing. They believed this kind of love to be dangerous and likely to burn out quickly unless supported with one of the less superficial loves. I cannot help but agree. Eventually those heated, first stage relationship days tend to ebb into a different vibration – committed love.

Something like what the Ancient Greeks dubbed *Pragma*. A hallmark of healthy, long-term relationships. Pragma is about giving love - patience, tolerance, and compromise - essential elements for a successful long-term relationship.

Still, I believe that passion is a super important component to any relationship. It is that initial burn of lust and desire that serves to fuel the love and begins to form the groundwork of the connection. Passion becomes the foundation upon which intimacy and deep love are born and nurtured; and love is the motivating law of life.

U.S Andersen expresses this perfectly when he said: *"The universe dances and sings and buds and blooms and builds. All of life clings to one another, serves one another in a great common purpose. Love pervades all, love is behind all, love is the great goal. Sex is life expressing love!"*

Even love on a train. Especially love on a train.

SEXUAL TRANSMUTATION AND ALCHEMY

Yesterday afternoon I stopped by the store to buy a bottle of wine. I was on way to my mother's place for a night away from home; away from the family. Mum time. She was cooking up a lamb roast. Obviously, we required a nice drop of wine to accompany such a dinner. So, I stopped by the store, selected the wine, which I chose based on the name plastered on the label. Does anyone else do this?

Well, it's the label along with my preferred flavor that influences my decision. For the wine connoisseurs out there reading this post, I'm mostly a Sauvignon Blanc woman. I figure my selection process is because I don't tend to buy and drink wine often. So, I never remember which ones I've liked and enjoyed previously. Yesterday, it was a cheerful looking label called *The Alchemists* that captured my attention ... and my imagination.

Alchemy: a seemingly magical process of transformation. How could I pass up on such a title? The silent promise of transformation via the fresh, vibrant flavors embodied in this citrus-infused drink proved too much to resist. Besides, Margaret River winery in Western Australia produces some quality wine – that, I remembered.

I plucked the bottle of magic from the fridge and made for the checkout counter where a couple were going about their transaction. A process that took FOREVER. For some reason, the woman was finding the payment method a challenge. Tap-and-go, honey. It's not so hard. I love the tap-and-go option. Quick. Easy. Efficient. Personally, I think it's one of the best innovations to arrive on the purchasing scene in recent years. That option means I can get in and out as fast as possible without screwing around with inserting cards and entering pin numbers. It's tap-and-go all the way for me.

There was no tapping-and-going happening that day, at least not for the couple in front of me. You know those times when you're waiting your turn at a checkout and the people in front of you glance your way a few times along with the checkout person? It's kind of awkward. You try not to appear as if you're waiting on them when the opposite is true.

In any case, it gave me enough time to notice the guy behind the counter – young, long brown hair pulled back and cinched at his nape with just the right amount of facial hair spreading across his jawline; a defined jawline, rugged and masculine, and startling blue eyes. He might've been just a little bit sexy, and I might not have really noticed the color of his eyes until the couple eventually shifted away and I stepped up to the counter.

"Just the wine?" he asked, smile emerging.

Avert eyes to wine bottle.

"Yep."

Smile breaks wide over fleshy lips. Eyes penetrate mine.

"Do you have a rewards card?"

"Nope."

I did, but I couldn't be bothered looking for it, especially with the incoming vibes southside of the counter. *Tap-and-go, honey.* Tap. And. Go.

I tapped, then:

"Would you like a paper bag?"

"Yes please," I replied, shoving my card back in my purse.

He passes me the now bagged wine bottle and the moment arrived. I looked at him, meeting his intense blue gaze for longer than a second for the first time, and you know what happened?

We both laughed.

Nothing unusually funny occurred during that simple transaction. No jokes were exchanged. It was the energy between us. The non-verbal communication playing out over a matter of minutes resulted in a mutual understanding and amusement. As it was, it was at that point that I blushed, thanked him and almost ran out of the store, feeling his vibes following me all the way to the car.

It got me thinking, though. We encounter so many people during our lives, yet with only a select few do we experience something more than ordinary. Why is that? What determines the variables between people that result in a meaningful encounter – even if only for a fleeting moment?

It is no secret that we are made of energy. Science today accepts that the universe – including us – is comprised of energy, not matter. This is not actually new – it was posited by Greek philosopher Socrates and by the ancient rishis in India thousands of years before that.

Socrates: *"Energy, or soul, is separate from matter. The universe is made of energy – pure energy – which was there before man and other material things like the Earth came along."*

This means that each moment of every day we are constantly emitting vibrations. If you are feeling positive, you will vibrate at a high frequency. When you are in a negative state of mind, your vibration mirrors that frequency and will only serve to bring you further down. The human energy system beyond the obvious physical layer includes subtle energy bodies: Etheric Body;

Emotional Body; Lower Mental Body; Higher Mental Body; Causal Body; Soul Body and the Integrated Spiritual Body. These invisible energy bodies vibrate at a slightly faster vibration than the one before it, culminating to form our Auric Energy Fields – the Etheric Body.

"What you seek is seeking you" – Rumi

Considering all this energy taking place in and around us, we are therefore constantly transmitting a frequency to the outer world, pulling toward us that which we broadcast. Think of it in terms of a magnetic field. Our vibration or energy influences the electric charges we transmit in relative motion – our magnetic field. The effects of our magnetic field attract or repel others.

The universal law of attraction – like attracts like.

Keeping that in mind, I'm not surprised about what had transpired between myself and the sexy checkout man, because honestly, during the drive to the store, my mind and energy was firmly placed on one of the most powerful and greatest motivational forces in life – sexual energy.

Yes, I might've been transmitting a heavy dose of sexual energy which he picked up on and responded to accordingly. I'm not ashamed, nor am I embarrassed to admit this. I'm a creative human being, and as a creative, sexual energy plays an important role in my work.

How? I hear you ask.

Did you know that our sexual energy is our creative, life-force energy? Through it, we give birth to new life.

Other than the obvious procreation sex produces (children), the same energy can be harnessed and channeled to give birth to new ideas and projects. Open and strong sexual energy contributes toward our vitality, creativity and sense of well-being.

In his book, *Think and Grow Rich*, Napoleon Hill states: *"Sex transmutation is simple and easily explained. It means the switching of the mind from thoughts of physical expression to thoughts of some other nature."*

This means that sexual transmutation is the process of converting sexual energy into some other drive, motivation, or energy of a higher order. The basis for sexual transformation is to take your sexual energy and channel it into a higher energy center. In short, healthy sexual energy can be crucial in fueling and producing amazing works of art.

I happened to be in the process of sexual transmutation that afternoon, which attracted a memorable moment with an attractive man. Something more than ordinary.

Well, that's my story and I'm sticking to it.

P.S. The bottle of Alchemy delivered, I was transported into another world, and today my head is cursing me for it.

WHO WANTS A VIRGIN ANYWAY?

"A houri is a beautiful young woman with a transparent body. The marrow of her bones is visible like the interior lines of pearls and rubies. She looks like red wine in a white glass. She is of white color, and free from the routine physical disabilities of an ordinary woman such as menstruation, menopause, urinal and offal discharge, child bearing and the related pollution. A houri is a girl of tender age, having large breasts which are round and not inclined to dangle. Houris dwell in palaces of splendid surroundings."

— Al-Tirmidhi

For some men bedding a virgin is an attractive prospect. Or so we are led to believe. Throughout Islamic mythology and Middle Eastern lore, the houris are full-breasted, dark-eyed nymphs untouched by man who will accompany the faithful in Jannah – the realm of the highest layer of heaven.

The Qur'an's heavenly vision focuses on luxury, leisure and sensual pleasures. In Islam, the idea of an afterlife filled with an abundance of polygynous sex with virginally pure partners refers to an aspect of paradise. Since we are sexual beings, God's provisions include everything believers need to be perfectly happy. For believing males this includes the very best sex possible.

Aside from all things made from heavenly misogynist delights, this line of thinking reflects across modern Muslamic practices today where virginity is defined as a piece of anatomy. An intact hymen is essential for a woman who wishes to be accepted into marriage. She also is expected to remain monogamous. Men on the other hand can engage in sex before marriage and are permitted to take up to four wives.

Besides the double standards blatantly displayed with the above-mentioned scenario, I have difficulty believing the polygynous lifestyle can be all that beneficial when it comes to forming and nurturing deep connection within a relationship. After all, isn't the whole purpose of a relationship based upon forging intimate bonds and complete fusion with another?

What would a man do with four wives anyhow? How would he meet and satisfy each of their emotional needs? Women are naturally emotional creatures. We thrive on deep emotional connection. We need to feel understood, seen and held by our partners. I am uncertain how my husband would cope should he have to contend with even twice the woman I am, let alone four of me.

But hey, if the wives all start out tender-aged virgins, then the male in question may have a lot less to navigate in the emotional-need department. Virgins may be considered submissive and easily domesticated. I can see how that works.

The idea of "breaking in" virgin females obviously fairs high on the priority scale in some cultures. In the Kanjarbhat ethnic group of India, newlywed brides are expected to submit themselves to a humiliating ritual – "The White Bedsheet Test."

Yes, it is as demeaning as it sounds. The bridegroom will take his bride along with a white bedsheet into a room while elders sit beyond the threshold awaiting the outcome - the moment for him to reappear and state whether or not the "product" was good. If his bride doesn't bleed, she can be subjected to beatings and communal humiliation.

Considering where I'm about to take this post, it is important to point out that I am not intending to make light of such degrading practices against women. On the contrary, the opposite is true. Gender inequality practices continue to take place around world and are in need of major adjustment. The fight for women's rights is far from over.

I was a virgin once. Yes, it is true. Like most of us, the moment my cherry was popped are among the moments forever burned in my memory - the low lighting in the room; the taste of his mouth; the way he held me close when he eased himself inside of me ... the sweet burning pain. And yes, there was blood; and then, I was no longer a virgin.

I was eager and curious to explore sex. There was no stopping us once I was introduced to my boyfriend's super-hard counterpart. Yet, as much as we screwed like bunnies facing the end of the world, sexual experience was a quality I had to cultivate.

Intercourse is not an instant pass into womanhood (or manhood for that matter). It takes many years of sifting and sorting through life – voyaging the diverse and often challenging experiences the journey dishes up before we fully realize adulthood.

Our sense of self develops and matures as we move through life to eventually arrive at a destination where we begin to own who we are and feel comfortable with that person – our sexuality plays a strong part in that evolution.

Women in particular battle an ingrained set of ideals on what it means to be sexually active. These are posited in a variety of ways at the onset – we are taught to be submissive in the bedroom through films, music clips and pornography. We are shown images of desirable women which causes countless hours of internal pain deliberating over our imperfections. We are subjected to being objectified, catcalled and judged by our appearance.

More often than not, the virgin female is unfamiliar with her intimate body and sexual desires. She lacks confidence in expressing that part of herself. She doesn't know what turns her on or how to ask her partner to do that thing she likes – she's still figuring that out along with her voice while he's intent on burning a hole through her panties every time she is near.

Of course, boys don't get off easy in the sexual experience sector. But they do seem to have a handle on what they want from the encounter. Their primal instincts rage for release - they just want to fuck. As long as our breasts are out for some not-so-gentle sucking and our legs are wide open, business is on. If we're lucky, we may score a little foreplay in the form of rough finger action before the main event.

Which inevitably ends with a trace dissatisfaction for us. Bury it with a sweet smile, babe. Tell him how hard you came and how much he pleases you. That's what we do, right? At least in the early years.

Women's bodies are made for love. We are curvy and sensual creatures with secretive places and seductive parts. Lips. Hips. Breasts. Delicate parts designed to give and receive pleasure that blossom when touched in just the right way. Seldom do those qualities come into full appreciation during the years when boys are looking to ramp up their hump-o-meter.

Fast forward to a mature man with sexual experience who has patience and stamina, and has learned to be an unselfish lover and I'll show you a man made of all things heaven.

The afterlife briefly described above is that of traditional Islamic beliefs and held by the vast majority of Muslims worldwide. So, what about the reward for the female believers when they reach paradise?

Apparently, the Qur'an seems to have little interest in it – women are not promised multiple virginal partners to frolic and fuck in the life thereafter. In fact, this idea would be considered offensive.

Perhaps it is just as well. I am certain women the world over would much rather have one soulful and well-seasoned man loving and appreciating her "offal discharge and related pollution" than an endless supply of inexperienced shags.

Bring on heaven.

SUPERHEROES

"My dream is to be a superhero and I will save people."
- Lakota

I clear an hour out of my schedule every other Monday morning to help in my son's kindergarten class. He loves it. The expression on his face every time I walk through the door is an impression that stays with me long after I've left.

His big brown eyes light up and with a big grin he rushes forward, throwing his arms around me as if he hadn't just seen me an hour before. He doesn't care who's watching either. I'm not sure how long that will last so I'll take it with a side of pleasure.

He is not the only one that loves it when I rock up ready to get my "silly" on. There's something about hanging out with a bunch of six-year-olds that refreshes and inspires the mind. Don't get me wrong; as much as I love it, I do so in small doses. I think teachers are like our modern-day superheroes.

This is going to sound a little creepy, but kid-watching can be extremely entertaining. We can learn so much from their zesty outlook, their resilient ability to go with the flow and their uncomplicated way of being. Those qualities are catchy.

So much so, that when I cross the threshold and into the classroom, I (almost) shed the invisible cords that bound me to adulthood and barely even acknowledge the teacher.

"My dream is to be a ballerina and I'll do a pirouette."
- Keira

I'm not like the other parent helpers. When those kids

show up at my bingo table, they know they're in for something different and a whole lot of laughs.

I am not just another mum flashing words and adhering to the "quiet-is-better" rule we get thrown down our throats every 10 minutes or so.

I am their "Bingo Master".

This self-proclaimed "Bingo Master" flashes word cards just like the other mums, but the other mums don't suddenly break out in a song using the word of the moment as a cue or playfully tease them when clutching words like "home" and "baby" in their hands. I give them challenges, dive into their imaginations and pluck out their fascinating ideas.

I ask the boys to draw love hearts and flowers, the girls' trucks and cars. Most boys screw their noses up at the thought of etching out a heart or a flower, but then I persist.

Other boys take their love hearts very seriously and need no further coaxing. Those boys are probably the ones set to change the patterns of love in the future. They are the ones who might seek out new relationship dynamics and boldly go where no one has gone before.

"My dream is to be a doctor and I will help people."
- Jack

Kids teach us so much about life. For instance, did you

know that Barbie dolls and unicorns can destroy a zombie apocalypse? And that helping yourself win on the sly isn't actually cheating? Moreover, kids teach us to see the world differently.

Their eyes are not yet contaminated by societal conventions and cultural conditioning. They remind us of sincerity with their transparent views and their beautiful curiosity. They remind us that everything is interesting, to live in the moment and to laugh at silly things. They remind us of our humanity.

> *"My dream is to be a teacher and I will teach kids."*
> *- Harley*

Children's dreams are like precious drops of light. In a world where dreams are too often squandered beneath doubt and ridicule, kids dream big and without boundaries. In a world where we're so afraid to love, kids love fiercely, forgive easily and listen to their precious hearts.

Every other Monday I spend time with my child and the children of others. Every other Monday, I leave that classroom feeling a little bit lighter than before I arrived.

If you're looking for a different way to kickstart your creative juices, go spend some time with kids. Go play, laugh and goof around a little. Breathe life back into those dreams and believe like a child again.

If just one thing would stick with me from the time I

spend with children, that would be it. To believe in those dreams with the voracity of a child again.

"My dream is to be a scientist and I will create a robot to cook me food when I'm hungry."
- Indiana

PARENTING IN THE FAST LANE

"I hate the world today!" Master Six said, scrunching his nose and treating me to a dark, brooding stare.

"Alrighty, that didn't take much," I replied.

Seriously, if putting on socks represented my greatest adversities, I'd take it in a flash. I tried not to smile, I really did, but when his rosebud lips began to curl my way, I failed miserably.

He has a thing for bums.

That wasn't a typo. Yep, the littlest man of the house has had a thing for the "butt" ever since he could walk and talk. I'm not sure why. Nothing out of the ordinary ever happened to erm... nurture this odd idiosyncrasy of his. Yet, he has this habit of dishing out a light paddle on behinds every now and then as he passes by. Namely, mine. Actually, only mine.

I've never seen him try it on his father. I'm thinking because my butt is much more padded than his dad's – which by the way, wouldn't take a whole lot to achieve. My husband has one of those behinds you can't see. Oh, you know it's there; it has to be – my senses remind me it exists more often than I'd like. It just seems to become swallowed in his clothes.

In my house, it isn't unusual to spot me randomly break out in my version of a booty dance while slapping my ass and crooning some of the lyrics to *Baby Got Back*. Well, the only part of the song I remember – *"I like big butts and I cannot lie; You other brothers can't deny."* Okay, I admit, it doesn't sound like a very mothery thing to do; swinging my hips and wriggling my behind at my children, but they laugh every time. I just hope they don't go searching up that song on YouTube any time soon.

Songs can be a good alternative to express ourselves sometimes. For instance, when I hear the words *"but it's not fair"* flung from one of my kid's mouths, I walk away singing The Rolling Stones classic *"You can't always get what you want"*. It's pretty self-explanatory. I tend to not elaborate after that, and they tend to not push the matter.

Unless we're in teenage territory, which is another ball game altogether. Her current song is *Teenage Dirtbag*. I know, it's not so adventurous, but if you could see some of the looks this princess saves just for me, you'd understand. I swear, I'm pretty sure she thinks I'm clueless. You know, adults, like, seriously have no idea about, like, anything. Especially when they croon those annoying words *"I'm just a teenage dirtbag, baby"* in your face, and don't understand why spending ridiculous amounts of money on acrylic nails is so important.

She doesn't laugh at my booty dance, by the way. No. She eye rolls and fluffs away into her cave where she spends an extraordinary amount of time on the crucial stuff – lying in bed and getting her social on. Those hours are paying off because the other day she showed us just how skillful she could be with her iPhone. She has cultivated the ability to blind-text. That's right, I watched as she watched me while her long, painted talons flew over the phone keypad as she produced a perfectly formed text message. It was oddly impressive. Until she told me it was the trick she uses in class.

"I can look right at the teacher and talk to her while texting beneath my desk, mum," she said, laughing.

What do you say to that when you know, given half the chance, it was something you would've done too? Of course, I didn't tell her as much. I managed to say the expected "motherly" things which do actually occur around here at times. It was promptly met with a smirk and a casual shrug before she pranced back into the den for more essential activities.

I took her shopping for her birthday recently. This is something for me because I hate shopping and she loves it.

My dislike for shopping isn't just limited to the mall. I hate all kinds of shopping. The mall, however, makes me feel giddy and light-headed after a while. Like I can't breathe. The food halls are the worst. *Argh*! Just the thought of being in that environment makes my skin crawl. All those people making noise and shuffling around the various food outlets before sitting down together to shovel it in their mouths ... no thanks. I'll pick up something to eat elsewhere and pray the kids have forgotten about McDonald's.

As if that will ever happen. Gross. Why do kids love that shit?

Teenage princess wanted her nose pierced for her birthday. After pretending to think about it for a few days, I decided to oblige and allow her to get a small shiny stud on one nostril. So, we went to the body-piercing shop and I watched as she braved the needle. Okay, I didn't really watch, I just stood at the threshold and gazed at the pictures on the walls while trying to appear supportive. I'm not into watching needles plunge into skin. I don't even watch when I get poked for blood tests.

It was over in a jiffy and without so much as a squeak from her. It looked kind of cute, too. Hmmm ... then came the lightbulb moment. I'm someone that tends to experience these spur-of-the-moment decisions from time to time. I don't always overthink everything. When I got my first tattoo, I had decided then and there and did it before I could procrastinate. Something similar happened that day when out with my daughter – I walked out of that mall with a brand-new sparkle adorning my left nostril. I, however, yelped during the process. Yep, turns out my teenage dirtbag is tougher than me.

For one glorious moment, I wasn't a clueless mother. I might've even been cool. My cool lasted for less than a week, though, because although I liked my little nose-stud, my subconscious mind rejected it. I ended up tearing it out during my sleep a few nights later and that hurt like hell.

"Go get it done again, mum," she said.

"No way."

"But it looked so cute on you." Blink, blink.

Yeah, I'll take the clueless mother tag and keep singing, sunshine.

ABUSE ME, ABUSE ME NOT

"Everything depends on your attitude towards yourself. That which you will not affirm to be true of yourself can never be realised by you, for that attitude alone is the necessary condition by which you realise your goal."
~ Neville Goddard.

I tend to never think about the past. For me, the past has served its purpose, and I know I will accomplish nothing if I choose to dwell over it. I'd rather look forward, focus on how I want life to be – not just only at the micro level, but at the macro level too.

Yes, I want to see change in the world, in humanity. I want to see a shift towards world peace, and I want to see every person act out of love and not fear. I'm not ashamed to admit that I am one of those dreamers John Lennon so famously sang about in his classic song, *Imagine*.

I am a dreamer. I have always been a dreamer. Even the darkest moments couldn't quite diminish the spark deep inside of me, and like many of us, I've lived through some dark times.

Relationships are a beautiful and necessary part of life. It is through our relationships and interactions with others that we learn so much about ourselves and the world. We learn great things like love, respect, empathy and consideration. We learn how to relate with others and the art of compromise. We fall in and out love, hearts break and we grow and evolve, and we realise what we do and don't want for ourselves.

Sometimes, those lessons are tough. Well, let's be honest, our biggest lessons are always the toughest to learn. The worst thing is when we get caught in a revolving-lesson door – the cycle drill that won't quit till you make a change in yourself. That was me.

I was on repeat – a lesson that began when I was sixteen years old and lasted until I finally kicked it in the butt when I reached thirty-four. That's right, almost twenty years of enduring one lesson through three relationships – abuse.

I am not a trained psychologist, nor have I earned any qualifications in social welfare. I have studied towards a Bachelor of Social Studies (psychology), earning two years of transcripts before I went on hiatus and began writing fiction books.

It was through study that I rediscovered my love of writing. I loved writing the essays for my modules, yet each of my lecturers had at some point mentioned the same thing upon reading my assignments – I wrote too creatively and needed to be more scientific, but hey, I wanted my work to be interesting, even when including the principles of clinical jargon and conventions. I loved writing books so much; the rest is history (excuse the cliché).

The point is, I don't traditionally qualify as a trained person to guide others going through abuse. But I do qualify as a domestic abuse survivor. I have experienced verbal and emotional abuse, physical and sexual abuse. Image abuse, and stalking.

I know how it feels to be that person – the one that lives behind closed doors in a world of shame; the one that beats herself up every day for her weakness; the person that can barely stand looking in the mirror because she failed herself and her children, and can't find a glimmer of light in a world of shadows.

For a long time, that was me. The worst thing about being a victim of abuse is the guilt that comes along with it. Guilt becomes a constant companion in a fake, plastic world. It's there when you wake up every morning, and it's there every second of pretending everything is okay.

There are all kinds of guilt – guilt for betraying your own convictions; guilt for convincing yourself it will never happen again while knowing full well it will, and finally, the guilt that eats you from the inside out – not protecting your beautiful children from the ridicule and violence.

Looking back, I guess I thought I didn't deserve any better. Sometimes, all it takes is one life-changing incident to set off a chain of events that can last a lifetime. I did it for almost twenty years.

I lived on my nerves and walked on eggshells, and every now and then I'd let loose and face the demons with a defiance I couldn't ignore – that spark deep inside of me flared to the surface and desperately screamed for justice, dignity and self-worth.

I know how it feels to have your life threatened. My first husband used to tell me that he would gladly do jail-time for my murder. Words enough to send a chill down my spine even recalling them.

I know how it feels to see the fault in yourself. What am I doing wrong? Why can't I do anything right? I'm a loser. I'm nothing.

And I know how it feels to see no way out of a black tunnel – "You couldn't survive without me, you wouldn't make it." "Nobody would want you, you're used goods." "You're useless, dumb, stupid, fat, ugly." "I'll use you up till there's nothing left."

Hear some things enough and you start to believe them.

So, what changed?

Me.

I'd had two little boys with my first husband, but it wasn't until we had a little girl that something really shifted in me. My little fair angel was the catalyst in a world of darkness. Maybe it was because of the time when my then husband pegged a TV remote controller at me when I was breastfeeding my newborn. He missed me but he didn't miss her.

Or perhaps it was how he'd ridicule me for not producing enough breast milk and our baby girl began to lose weight fast – my fault. Or maybe it was the times when he came home late at night drunk and woke me just to terrorise me.

Whatever it was, I knew I could no longer live that life. I knew there was more, much more, and that life was supposed to be happy.

I could find happiness. I could. I wanted more for my children. I wanted peace for them. I wanted to see them laugh more and make a mess if they wanted. I wanted them to feel confident and to know a better existence.

I remember one night I went outside and gazed at the stars. I looked and looked until I believed in something higher than myself. I asked for strength, guidance and courage, and I knew if my life was going to change it would be up to me to make the change. No one would do it for me. No one.

So, I did it. I took a breath and summoned my courage. I got a house and packed our stuff and with the help of some beautiful friends, I moved myself and my children out of that situation and I never looked back.

Not once – even when he begged me to come home, or when things got tough and he made life difficult. Control is not something people easily relinquish. I was out and it was the best thing I'd ever done.

The thing is, I chose myself. I chose my children. And I chose to believe in those stars. Somehow, I knew everything would be okay. I took a leap of faith, and even though it wasn't always easy going, I still chose to believe. It would take another five or more years for me and my children to sift through the emotional scars that that environment left on us.

There were challenging times dealing with adolescents with major anger issues; there was heartache and tears, feelings of hopelessness and working through the guilt. But we got through it together, and my children were my salvation and I was theirs.

I still gaze at the stars and I still believe in them. I know for a fact the abilities I possess to initiate the changes I desire in my life because I've done it, and I know that the power comes from within, and not from outside of myself. It's in all of us.

If you want change, only you can make it happen. And if you don't want to get stuck in the revolving-lesson door, you *need* to adjust the way you think regarding the specific subject. One of my favourite Wayne Dyer quotes is when he said, "Change the way you look at things, and the things you look at change."

Those words resonate with me so much, I wrote them down and stuck it on the wall next to my bed to remind me that no situation is immovable, no matter how static or impossible it seems.

Choose happy. Choose yourself. And please don't focus too much on those dark times you experienced in the past – give power to the future you desire and be a dreamer like John Lennon. Imagine.

SOME APOLOGIES ARE ENDLESS

When I was a teenager my friends and I spent many hours discussing futuristic relationships. Secrets smiles and girly giggles accompanied much of these conversations. Dreams floated somewhere above us encased within invisible pink bubbles tied with crimson ribbons; the man of our dreams awaited to sweep into our lives when the universe conspired our fated meeting. We could barely wait.

Dreams.

They are the cornerstone of imagination and make the world go around. They form the wings of precious wishes and exquisite desires, and there are none so much as precious as the promising dreams of love to a girl.

My teenage dreams foretold love like no other – he was charming and smart, caring and tender; his smile would light up my heart and quicken my pulse. He was open-minded, sweet and compassionate. He was witty, vulnerable yet strong. Most of all, though, he respected me.

Respect.

This quality was vital and posed lengthy in-depth discussions among our group. None of us had a history of violent homes, yet we were more than aware of the widespread violence against women that went on behind closed doors.

My convictions were strong; I would never tolerate violence or mistreatment from my future partners. Never.

But the convictions of a girl who dreamed of falling in love fizzled as time moved forward to present a man who she thought possessed the above qualities. They say love is blind. Perhaps it is. But I think that an open-heart nurtures forgiveness, tolerance and empathy, and it is those elements of love that can become the foundation under which the narcissist to thrive.

She was giddy. Excitement filled her. The future stretched untouched and perfect beneath his devotion. They would stick together through thick and thin; they would carve the path and create dreams. They would love and be loved. Hold and be held.

But dreams are nothing when the edges begin to crack and the shadows start to loom.

Excitement fades when the constant barrage of demeaning comments begin chip at your psyche. The convictions of a girl drown in a tsunami of guilt when he kicks you so hard that you can barely walk for a week, or tells you he would gladly do jail time for your death.

"I'm sorry, honey. I'll make it up to you."

Some apologies are smothered in gold jewels, international holidays and new clothes. Some even take on the form of a new car.

Thwack!

"I was feeling a little cagey – you stepped on my toes. I'm sorry, honey. It will never happen again. I love you."

Some apologies are made from delusion even when delivered sincerely.

Goodbye dreams. So long, respect. Enter guilt, self-loathing and everything black. Black for the single most horrific day that still haunts me – the day the screams of my little boys followed me down the hall as he gripped my scalp and dragged me to the bedroom. Black for the moments my heart split when they watched from the threshold as he flung me on the bed and punched me in the head. Black for the terrified eyes that blinked back at me.

Boom!

My ears throbbed and my head pounded. The sound of his voice reverberated somewhere in the distance as he growled. But I felt nothing and heard nothing as I focused on the horrified eyes brimming from the doorway.

Some moments you can never undo. Some moments stay with you no matter how deep you bury them.

I'm sorry for the charred dreams and teenage wishes

snatched away by brutality. I'm sorry for betraying the convictions and values that I had so strongly believed in. I'm sorry for abandoning my sense of self-respect, self-love and self-worth. Most of all, I'm sorry for the innocence stolen away from my little boys the day their world turned black.

Some apologies are never too late to be expressed. And some apologies last forever.

FRIENDSHIP IS LIKE TREASURE

I have a friend. Her name is Sharon, but I call her Shaz. She was born in Johannesburg, South Africa but she's really Scottish. Luckily for me, her family migrated to Australia a few years before we met during my first year of high school.

Shaz is like a breath of fresh air on a sweltering day. She's grounded and practical, yet also open to new ideas and alternative possibilities. She can make me laugh till I cry and my cheeks ache, yet she has an extremely sensible disposition. She's also a dreamer. Artistic and creative at heart, her brushworks are extraordinary and she's smart – numbers are her thing and she excels at it.

What I like most about Shaz are her gentle and positive qualities. She has this beautiful, calming energy and she's as loyal and patient as they come. And when it comes to me, she doesn't play games or mince words, even when it comes to delicate matters. She has a way of expressing the truth without cutting to the bone. I love that about her. Seldom will she allow anger or frustration to influence her reactions, and this was true of her nature even when we were kids.

I can always count on her honesty. I hate guessing games and fart-assing around, so I guess we suit each other. Generally, we all like to know where we stand with others. With Shaz, I know where I've stood, still stand and will always stand. In turn, she knows where she stands with me.

We've had our differences over the years. Like, how best to cook baked beans. Yes, that's as far and as heated as our disputes have ventured. We were 16 years old and she was holidaying with my family on the Gold Coast. The debate got heated that day. We stalked from the kitchen in opposite directions and didn't talk for hours following that argument. Baked Beans almost ruined a good friendship, but it didn't. Good friendships practice forgiveness.

Shaz is an excellent listener. She'll listen until there's nothing left, then she'll offer an opinion if asked. Let me tell you this about Shaz. Her guidance and advice never originates from a self-satisfying or judgmental position. She has this ability to see a situation from all angles, keeping the bigger picture in mind and still often surprises me with her insightful suggestions.

Good friends have our backs when life gets tricky and keep our stress in check.

Good times.

We flew to New York city once and spent a week exploring together before parting ways – she on a pre-booked North American tour, while my sights were set on a trip to Canada. We'd spent the week sharing a hotel room the size of a peanut and sleeping in a double bed that caved in the middle beneath our weight.

That's another of Sharon's abilities; she can sleep soundly even in the most uncomfortable circumstances. I've always envied this about her. Then again, she didn't have to listen to herself snoring through the night....

On our second last night in New York, we had recovered enough from jetlag, sightseeing and shopping to hit the town. We had a plan – we would start out some place near Times Square and make our way through as many bars across the city as we could squeeze in. A NY bar-crawl.

Woop!

Out came the heels and lipstick; in came the delicious alcoholic sour concoctions served up at our first stop, an Irish bar called the Playwright. Truth is, we never had a chance at that planned bar-crawl. It began and stopped right there, in a cozy little bar on West 49th. Yep, we got talking with the barmaid, the charming Irish owner named PJ, the locals and the drop-ins, and it wasn't long before we'd settled in for a night of – well – you know.

That night was packed with laughs, unusual proposals and surprises. I was asked out on two dates, hit on by a local hustler, rescued by the bar staff and offered a bed if I agreed to ditch my Canadian plans and instead stay a week longer in New York – thanks PJ. A guy from the NBC asked me to join him in the basement for a couple of lines of coke, and my foot was savagely squished and injured by Sharon's heel when, at the end of the night, we raced through our extraordinary long hotel corridor toward our door in an effort to secure the bathroom first. I think I lost.

I could barely move the next day, and it wasn't because of my swollen foot. Last day in New York city and I spent it in bed nursing the hangover from hell while Shaz took a helicopter ride over the Hudson river, almost puking mid-flight. Heee!

Early next morning I left her standing on the sidewalk in a foreign city as I set off for LaGuardia airport. That was one of those moments that stick with you. I'd said goodbye to her a million times before that, but that time was different. That time it felt more profound.

Good friends accept us for who we are during the good and bad times. Good friends don't expect, demand, manipulate or control.

I had another friend once. I loved her. But she was too controlling. She gave me ultimatums when my choices didn't suit her. She'd tell me how long I could keep a man in my life, for example - husband.

My current husband and I had a rocky start. Passionate, yes, but our union resembled a spinning yo-yo for the first few months. Round three, and this friend gave me the hard word – him or me. I mean, whaaaat?

Umm .... see ya, hun. I'm not in the business of ultimatums. My life, my choice. Family members do the same kind of thing. My brother stopped talking to me too. When he realized my man had really manned-up, was sticking around and in it for the long haul, he backtracked and turned his decision into something else. I talk to our mother, you see. He doesn't. Another story, same shit. His hang-up, not mine.

Good friends are respectful and supportive.

Regardless of the personal choices you make in your life, a genuine friend will support you through adversity. They'll also tell you when you're being a dick, but they won't use emotional blackmail as a means of control. Good friends won't bring you down or try to hurt to you, but they'll keep you humble. They will celebrate your accomplishments and remind you of your roots. They will uplift you, and in turn, you do the same for them.

Real friendship knows no time.

There have been long stretches of time when Shaz and I haven't spoken. Not because we've had a disagreement, simply because life happens. You know you've found a good friend when time means nothing. When you can pick up the phone after a year and talk as if you've spoken yesterday. That's the kind of people I want in my life.

In Shaz I know how fortunate I am to experience the rich and beautiful friendship that began in high school and continued to grow and strengthen with me over the years. I must have done something to score a friend like her, I must have.

CHANGE – WHAT LIGHT'S YOU UP ON THE INSIDE?

"Love is friendship set on fire."
~ Jeremy Taylor

What lights you up inside?

Have you ever looked back and imagined your entire life as chapters of a book? And that each chapter began with an inciting incident that eventually led to a critical point that became that one moment when you stood at a crossroads? You remember that one – the time when you knew your decision would determine the way your life would unfold over the months and years to follow.

Of course, we experience more than one of those pivotal moments during a lifetime. It's how it's meant to be; how we grow and evolve as individuals and as a species. Besides, life would fast become mundane if we were not periodically presented with new possibilities. It's as if the universe peels back to reveal a crack every now and then – a sliver wide enough to illuminate a path brimming with alternative prospects of a different life.

Our bellies may flutter as we peek through the doors of a mysterious future. We might slide on our dark shades to peer into the uncharted hours of a life spreading before us like the light of the moon trailing across the ocean's surface. Thinking ... pondering ... mulling over the would-be path while we analyse and sift through the possibilities until we decide whether to embrace something different or stay put and play it safe.

Sometimes, it might be a work opportunity or a crazy idea that entails a certain amount of risk. Other times, it might be more personal life choices like love and relationships where the stakes are raised high enough to warrant a vault pole if we decide to take a leap of faith. Whatever the moment is, one thing you can count on is that it will usually show up when you least expect it.

It's easy to resist change. After all, the future is unpredictable and uncertain. No one can really foretell what the future holds; freewill takes care of that. Gifted psychics and mediums can only take you so far. Their visions are always confined by a higher order. In other words, those intelligent beings existing in the higher realms looking out for you will only allow you to uncover so much about the future. The rest is left solely to your own discovery in order to strengthen your personal growth and life lessons.

Makes sense. If we knew without a doubt the events yet to unfold, how would we really be able to relish those moments as we experience them? We wouldn't, and that's the beautiful mystery of life – to be present and participate fully; to feel and resonate with our emotions as our paths wind through rocky waters and soar at wonderous heights, and to anchor ourselves in the present while keeping a firm vision of our ambitions and desires in our mind's eye.

And this is why the present is all-powerful, because the present is all we have to ground our feet in deep and practice assuming that our desires are fulfilled before we leap into the future. Does this not excite you as it does me? That your dreams and aspirations, desires and hunger to create are as real as you want them to be; as real as the power *you* decide to extend to them. The energy will always go where it is directed so direct it wisely.

I love the way Neville Goddard expresses this notion in his book *The Power of Awareness* when he states, *"All transformation begins with an intense burning desire to be transformed. You must want to be different before you can begin to change yourself. Then you must make your future dream a present fact. You do this by assuming the feeling of your wish fulfilled."*

We can't stop change from happening. Even when we think nothing is changing, it always is. The invisible wheels are always shifting in the background of our lives. We change even when we don't want to change – physically and emotionally, our circumstances, environment and relationships. So, if our lives are always changing, why not embrace the all-powerful present to manipulate your future into your most burning desires?

If we're being honest here, it is through our relationships that offer us the most value on the everchanging wheel-deal. This is where things can get tricky when thinking about our future, but without those rich and transformative experiences relationships provide, we cannot reach our full emotional potential as evolving human beings.

We are mothers and fathers, sisters and brothers, aunts, uncles, grandparents, friends and lovers. We wear many hats for many different people. Each relationship has its own authentic current pertaining to the two individuals involved; each provides layers and experiences that enrich our lives in some way, even when we are confronted by conflict within those connections. Yet, of all the relationships we experience, it is through the ones we connect with at the heart that really shape and cultivate our lives – the ones that burn like an exquisite flame to light us up on the inside.

Have you ever felt your breath thin and your heart explode when confronted by that special someone? Or told someone that they were the best part of your day and meant every word?

Love. Messy, scary, exciting, beautiful love. Everyone experiences it differently, and each time it happens, it is never the same as the time before. Anyone that has experienced it knows it is the best feeling ever. Love is like a rainbow; even when it's not returned, it is still filled with glorious colors that shade your heart with beauty. Love is never wrong. *Never*. But the thing about love is that it is subjective and intangible, and it's different for us all.

It can grow and flourish, making us feel smitten, crazy happy and utterly delirious with all things wonderful. And sometimes, it can take a turn and produce the opposite effects – it can sour and hinder your happiness, clip your wings and make you sad. Sometimes, love just runs its course for the length it takes for that relationship to reach its full potential. This is when the two in question become passive within the connection; when they no longer challenge and fuel one another at the deep levels required in order to continue evolving and learning from the union.

I know this situation well. We probably all have at some point or another. Remember earlier when I mentioned imagining the everchanging sections of our lives like chapters of a book? Here's the super-short version of one long chapter in my life, and it all started with a guy…

Love was the ***inciting incident***. I fell in love with a guy I had known during my childhood years. He reappeared into my life like a lovely blonde vision with a cute smile and a gentle demeanor, and every part of me succumbed to his blue-eyed, boyish charm. Yep, I totally melted while my heart sang and other parts went wildly crazy. It wasn't long before he took me to the beach, produced a diamond and asked for my hand in marriage. Truth be told, it scared the bejesus out of me. I was 21 years old with plans to travel and see the world before thinking about marriage. But he was so damned vulnerable and sincere in that moment that I couldn't bear the thought of turning him down.

My bad.

The usual entailed; we set out to make a life together. We moved around a bit until eventually buying a house, cars and furniture; a cat came along ... then children. Travel emerged too. We cruised the south Pacific, visiting cool places like Vanuatu, Fiji and New Caledonia. We flew to New Zealand to spend time with his Kiwi family, and he bought me stuff – lots of stuff. I was buried beneath so much stuff, I didn't know what to do with it.

Hmm.

Progressive complications are ... well ... complicated. Not all things are what they appear to be. Come to think of it, most things aren't what they appear to be. On the outside we *appeared* to be the perfect family. Lots of stuff and travel makes for a convincing veil. Yet there is truth to that old saying about what happens behind closed doors. You know those kinds of people that don't possess the ability to recognize their own toxic behavior and the effects it has on others? They are the worst kinds of bullies because you cannot reason with them no matter how much you try.

I tried hard.

For many years I over-stayed my welcome in a marriage with thoughts of making it work. I was really kidding myself, but we're all pretty good at that, right? The idea of change was terrifying. There was our jointly owned home to consider, combined assets and finances, and of course, the cat and the children.

Life happens...

The months turned into years and more years, and I knew in my core that that relationship could no longer serve me in the ways I yearned to be served. The connection had faltered, waned and had become a shadow of the beginning. I longed to be able to connect at a meaningful level; needed to relate and expand in ways that he was unable to reach – through soul, spirit, intellect. Which naturally spills over into producing the ultimate bedroom experiences, by the way.

Sigh.

We all do the best with what we have and what we are capable of in the moment. It took me a while to realize that he wasn't capable of taking a hard look at himself and readjusting accordingly at that time in his life. But these were my lessons too, and I strongly believe that we never get more than what we can take.

I took a lot, and lots of stuff doesn't come close to filling the void within.

This really was nobody's fault. He was physically and emotionally abusive, controlling, and extremely difficult to live with. Yet, that was *his* hang up; his own demons that would become his undoing. In the early years before we had children, there were times when he would lock me in our apartment before he'd go to work his night shift. He would lock me in there with no way out, only to return home and demand to inspect my nether region.

Was it fresh, plump and pink this day? Or had it taken a serving?

God forbid had I decided to serve myself while the cat was away. Have you ever been subjected to that line of questioning as someone has their nose buried between your legs with a microscope in hand?

"Uh-hum, it appears you are somewhat swollen." Dark frown raises with suspicion. *"Who's been here?"*

"Huh? Are you out of your mind?"

Yeah, someone was losing it and I'm certain it was me. He actually didn't have a microscope, but considering the amount of effort he put into this inspection, he may as well have. Besides feeling utterly violated at such a derogatory treatment, I had no idea how he thought another man could get in. Too bad if the building caught fire too. I would've been toast.

The **Crisis** eventually arrived in the form of suffocation. Over the years our relationship had disintegrated to the point of disparity and existed for the sake of familiarity, the vows we had taken and the children we had created. Discordance dominated the connection; the pages in our book were verging on an entirely different series. Emptiness replaced the meaningful exchanges and delicious intimacy we had once thrived on – and yes, that was there in the beginning. But intimacy and connecting had become something of the past and I needed more for myself, and yet, I buried that internal need to grow for the longest of times.

The universe offered a crack. I had a choice.

If I continued to play it safe, I would be better off financially and the children would not have to endure the reality of a broken home. Stay and I wouldn't have to endure hardship or raise three children alone; stay and I would remain miserable and oppressed, and in doing so, I would inevitably deny myself of my own truth.

Climaxes are not always earth-shatteringly exquisite, but they always bring change. I'm not certain what finally broke the final piece of resistance, but suddenly, something clicked inside of me – I couldn't deny what I needed and craved in order to nourish my soul. It was then that I began the change by anchoring myself in the present and daring to see my life differently; a life that he had spent years trying to convince me that I was too weak to create.

So, one day when he was condemning and criticizing me, I looked him in the eye and told him that he could try as hard as he liked but he would NEVER break me. Then I did it – I made the first moves to make a change that I had thought was nearly impossible.

He wasn't an easy man to escape. Those who thrive on controlling women never are. He even threw things at me as I held my terrified two-year-old and stuffed my belongings in boxes as I prepared to shift myself and my children out of there.

Resolutions are like a breath of fresh air as the new normal settles in your bones. I had resisted change because I was afraid of the unknown, but it was when I peeked through the crack the universe had provided for long enough that I believed that I was able to place my faith in an uncharted future. It was either that or continue on the same path that *wasn't lighting me up on the inside*. And that is what it comes down to – knowing when to embrace the mysteries of an unmapped future and when to play it safe.

The future is there regardless. Playing it safe and hiding from exciting opportunities or unbridled passion, or just a change for the better might be terrifying, but it won't enrich your life in the same ways that owning your truth will. We are here to carve our notch on the surface of time.

If we don't write our chapters with our authentic selves, then we cheat ourselves more than anyone.

It's like being faced with a field of blooming daisies and the universe cracks open to present you a rare wildflower. Picking the wildflower could be risky and exhilarating, but it could mean the beginning of the next chapter in your life if you are but game and brave enough to pluck the stem from the universe and step into the uncharted future.

HEARTBEAT – A WOMAN'S RIGHT

Outrage. Annihilation. Protest. Eradication.

*H*ate me.

I have exercised my rights as a woman to make decisions concerning my body, my health, the quality of my life and that of my family. I have opted to terminate a pregnancy. Twice.

Did you know that it is estimated that one in four pregnancies worldwide end in an abortion every year? That means the need for this basic healthcare is crucial for millions of girls and women across the world, and yet, access to safe and legal abortion services is far from guaranteed for those who may be in need of such services.

Are you cringing yet?

I get it, I really do – abortion falls under the taboo topic for many people. Gets them all fidgety and uncomfortable-like. I wonder if those are the same folks that squirm when confronted with stuff like gay and lesbian rights, gender equality or racism. Okay, maybe I actually don't get the cringing...

I don't tend to watch the news either. At all. This can quite possibly be considered ludicrous behavior in this day and age, but it is true. I have deliberately chosen to not keep up-to-date and informed on the latest catastrophes and negative events constantly circulating in the world, and I have survived just fine for twelve years without it.

I'm a firm believer in choosing what I allow into my experience. When I watch something that is disturbing, I'm inviting the essence of that into my inner-world – my sacred sanctuary. For instance, it affects me deeply when I witness the hate, suffering, violence and war infecting the earth. And mostly, I want to feel good as much as I can, so I try to avoid whatever brings discord. That might be considered selfish on my part, but sometimes we need to be a little selfish in order to protect ourselves.

I didn't need to hear the newsflash about the girl that was dismembered and stuffed into a suitcase. And I definitely didn't need to know about the outrageously absurd "Heartbeat" abortion laws denouncing women's rights. But some things don't slip past my radar. Unfortunately.

The Heartbeat abortion law effectively outlaws the procedure after six weeks of pregnancy. Pam Belluck from The New York Times, *"These so-called "Heartbeat" laws ban abortion after the point when a fetal heartbeat can be detected. This often occurs as early as six weeks into a pregnancy, when an ultrasound may be able to detect the pulsing of what will become the fetus's heart."*

At first, I thought it might be a sick joke played out by some over-privileged, chauvinistic male politician with a mundane haircut and a nose like a snout. Turned out, I was wrong (at least, on some counts). I mean, six weeks? There is actually no heart to beat in a six-week embryo. A tiny cluster of cells and pulsing tissue doesn't constitute a heart.

Who actually knows they're pregnant before the six-week marker for certain, anyway?

A lot of pregnancy tests fail to pick up on the elevated HGH (human growth hormone) levels in the system that early on – and trust me I know; I've been pregnant eleven times. Yep, you could say I used to be a very fertile woman. All I'd have to do is flutter some dark bedroom eyes toward my partner and bam – there was some funky, cell-clustering, tissue-pulsing action going on, and I'm not talking about the orgasmic variety either. That part happened prior to the big bang.

The same isn't true these days because I exercised another of my human rights and *chose* to undergo an endometrial ablation – a surgical procedure that destroys the lining in the uterus, and therefore I can no longer become pregnant. I killed cells and living tissue; is that illegal too?

Sexual and reproductive rights mean we should be able to make our own decisions about our own bodies. Yet all over the world many of us are persecuted for making our own choices and many more are prevented from making any choices at all. Last time I checked, we weren't living in the Stone Age. Surely time is not spiraling in the other direction toward a primitive ethos hanging between the legs of cowering cowards? Haven't women suffered enough beneath misogynist perspectives designed to appease self-gratifying ambitions to exert dominance over us?

Women and girls continue to suffer at the blunt end of an archaic bludgeon in many ways and in so many countries across the world. But it is delusional to think that preventing us from accessing an abortion does not mean we will stop needing one. Attempts to ban or restrict abortions will accomplish nothing but to force people to seek unsafe alternatives.

I have given birth to five healthy babies, lost four more through miscarriage, and chosen to abort two pregnancies. That is a freedom of choice I rightly own as a woman *and* a human being; a freedom born to me, and that right shouldn't have to be entrusted to or dictated by any government or religious deity.

Enduring a miscarriage is difficult; I have experienced the loss, heartache and the emotional pain that accompanies miscarriage. It stays with you for a long time. During the aftermath, you battle wretched feelings of failure and inadequacy, and you wonder if that somehow you did something wrong, that you deserved to lose the pregnancy.

But if anyone assumes that choosing to undergo an abortion is any less difficult than a naturally occurring abortion, than they would be a mistaken.

The fact is, choosing to abort a pregnancy does not come lightly; it does not come without first dredging into your soul and searching your heart; and it does not come without consequences. It has seen me plunge into the depths of depression and despair that was so dark, I couldn't see a pin-drop of light for the longest of times.

So, I ask, do you think a decision like that is taken with a grain of salt? That an experience like that is easily forgotten?

For every woman and girl that chooses to have an abortion, I can almost guarantee the same holds true for each of them. We don't need to be judged for our choices; we already do that enough for ourselves. We don't need anyone to make us feel ostracized or guilty either; we've got that covered too. And we don't need to be forced to sneak around to find dirty backstreet clinics run by a sleazy guy with a rusty hook and risk our lives in order to exercise a right that belongs to us.

I am not necessarily a feminist activist. I don't participate in outrage culture. Hell, I don't even watch the news. But I am woman, and every woman knows how it feels to be a woman in today's world; every woman knows the struggles we face as women, and the lack of equality that still lingers. Sometimes, some us have to speak up.

Taking away our rights and personal choices as women is wrong. It's just wrong.

GO AHEAD, BE OFFENDED. YOU HAVE THAT RIGHT

BY XAVIER EASTENBRICK

Being a man often means I must accept the fact that men have (arrogantly) made all kinds of decisions affecting women. Many of which were designed and intended as a means of control. Generally speaking, they were designed and intended to forbid women from exercising equal rights and privileges men enjoy because of a deeply flawed sense of paternalism. This decisional oddity is reflective of the culture of the time. I accept this as an historic reality; a reality that was ripe for change.

We live in an age where the situation appears to be improving, but unfortunately it isn't equal. The dynamics of the abortion debate are often difficult and messy, because we make it so. It is even difficult for both sides of the discussion to use the same language when talking about their positions. Unfortunately, the law and decisions surrounding the issues often further complicates the matter.

Separate and apart from the respective sides of the discussion, the sub-debate on abortion is whether men should have any say in the matter because it's not their body.

The history surrounding the issue of abortion has been dominated by the voices of men in the United States until the Supreme Court determined that it is the woman's right to choose. That is settled law and regardless of political movements to change the law, it is highly doubtful such attempts would survive constitutional scrutiny, at least in the United States.

At the same time, putting aside principles of constitutional law, if a couple are considered as one in the eyes of God (using a religious view) and the government (the legal view which is reflective of the religious view), shouldn't a decision about a life created by two people within that union, be a matter of qualified agreement to some degree during the pregnancy? After all, the law recognizes rights of fit biological parents once the child is born.

I'm going to say something which may seem controversial, only because of the ongoing societal debate. *Life begins at conception.* That should be an accepted scientific fact. Life even exists prior to the sperm fertilizing the egg, but upon conception, mitosis follows and the process of the human embryo begins. If it is left alone and assuming no other factors, natural or otherwise interrupt it, that embryo will turn into a human fetus and be born a baby.

All of those words describe a part of the process and development of human life. However, it is all still human life - a separate life and distinct from its mother, regardless of whether it could survive on its own.

The argument that it isn't a life unless it can survive on its own is a rather dangerous and slippery slope. If you put a baby on a hill and left it alone, it will likely die because it cannot survive in its own. *Is a life any less alive in utero than outside the womb, if neither could survive on their own?*

Here's something that may shock you; the fact that it is a life is not the end of the discussion for me. So, you understand this isn't some kind of academic debate. Allow me to discuss my personal experiences involving my ex-wife that occurred within our eleven-year marriage.

Early on, my wife and I became pregnant. Of course, she was the one carrying but the life inside her was *ours*. That isn't some antiquated notion of paternalism or latent misogyny. *She didn't become pregnant by way of a visit from an archangel.* Having said that, it turned out that my swimmers were way too eager and fertilized the egg in her fallopian tube, resulting in an ectopic pregnancy.

The doctors told us that there was no chance that the

fetus would develop or be born, and that if we did not abort, my wife could go into shock and die.

No brainer, right?

After two shots of methotrexate, the HGC (Human Growth Hormone) levels in my wife's system remained elevated, posing a danger to my wife. It had to be surgically removed. What entailed was a traumatic experience. My wife bore the brunt of the pregnancy and the burden it brought - complications, medication and surgical procedures. I was essentially a supportive and passive bystander who paced a waiting room and did what I could to attend to her needs.

About a year later, we found out that we were pregnant again with our son. He is now 9 years-old. Success, from conception to delivery. There wasn't a decision to be made about whether he would be born. He was a life with whom we interacted before he was born. Legally speaking, she could have terminated him and there would be nothing I could have done to stop her.

About a year later, we were pregnant again. When we went for the ultrasound, we were thrilled when we found out that she was carrying twin girls. We saw them on the monitor and heard their heartbeats. **They were no less alive than our son.**

Later, the doctor needed to talk with us because there was a potentially serious complication. The girls were monoamniotic monozygotic twins. That's a complicated way of saying that they were identical twins, and instead of two occupying separate amniotic sacs inside my wife's womb, they were developing in one sac together.

This is a dangerous situation because of the risks of cord strangulation. The doctor explained the risks - explaining that we (she) could choose to terminate the pregnancy. We discussed the matter, agreeing that our twins deserved a chance at life.

We didn't debate what these two lives were or whether my wife had a right to choose or whose bodies they were growing in. We wanted to afford our daughters their fair chance to live. Their fate was initially in our hands, but no more than the fate of our infant son. In our son's case, his birth means that he is protected by the law as a free human life and we, as his fit parents are both legally responsible for him.

June 3rd, 2011 and twenty-six weeks into the pregnancy, a routine ultrasound revealed that our twins had died. I'll never forget that day. I was working in NYC and received a call from my wife with the devastating news. Right away, I grabbed my things with no desire to talk to anyone, leaving the most brutal email I have ever composed and sent to my supervisor; *"My twins died. I left to be with my wife."* The train ride home was a blur, and not once had I debated whether those girls were a "life". We lost our daughters. We didn't lose feti.

The umbilical cords were irretrievably tangled around

their necks. The potential danger became a horrible reality. One died and then the other. On June 5th, 2011 they were officially "born" - if that's the right word. I will spare you the gruesome details. But what I saw that day, I will never forget.

My wife went through the hell of the delivery. My hell was psychological; to see her going through the painful labor, and then watch my daughters born dead, strangled in an unholy mesh of once life-sustaining umbilical cords.

What you might not know is that after 24 weeks, the hospital does all of the normal things that occur during a birth, except instead of a birth certificate, they issue a death certificate.

If you are at a hospital and see a picture of a purple flower on the door of a delivery room, please say a silent prayer for the poor souls experiencing a quiet and unspeakable journey through a highly personal hell. I often wonder what kind of strange laws created this anomaly of having died, but also never having been born. I suspect it is the result of people not wanting to acknowledge a life in the womb is a life. Once you call it "life", people who are not invested in that life assume they need to make decisions for the lives of all involved.

To recap and to better understand my opinion; I have participated in pregnancies - the necessary termination of one, the birth of another and the death of our twin girls. My wife didn't get pregnant alone, nor did she decide alone. It was her right to do so and I fully recognize that, but the decisions were made by us. If I had the ability to be pregnant and/or bear her pain, I would have, but that's not how biology works. I am a man; she is a woman and no debate will change the process of procreation.

It is interesting how these experiences have molded my perspectives. Having grown up Roman Catholic, I was always taught to be rigidly prolife. It was a matter of religious dogma, not subject to debate. As I matured, life also guided me. As a younger man, I watched my grandmother who had showed me how to love unconditionally, suffer with Alzheimer's. I could only watch her slow torture at the hands of that horrible disease. Until a stroke ushered her death, but not before paralyzing half of her body and stealing virtually all of her memories.

Later, my father would suffer the same fate, except mercifully be taken by pancreatic cancer. That's how bad Alzheimer's is; that cancer was a blessing.

What was the state of their "lives" in the end?

I'm not going to debate the issue of euthanasia or assisted suicide; however, my point is that they were not able to live without extraordinary medical intervention. No one would argue that my family had the right to terminate their lives, only because they were born.

However, in my father's case, my mother was his healthcare representative. When my father, riddled with Alzheimer's and cancer, and who also had a heart condition, the doctors recommended a pacemaker be installed. She discussed my father's options with my brother, sister and me, and wisely decided not to prolong his journey with extraordinary means. She remembered my grandmother, who had a pacemaker installed 20 years prior, and who also went through the entire horrible journey of Alzheimer's. She spared my father from that fate. My father wouldn't have wanted to live that way.

Put aside the legal discussion surrounding the abortion issue for a moment because nothing I say will sway a court of competent jurisdiction, or even move the needle of society's momentum in general to agree with my viewpoint.

That having been said, **what if we were to fairly and equitably create a societal standard to guide the rights of those affected by a pregnancy, and instead of a purely liberty based standard, we introduced an element of responsibility?**

The first thing introducing responsibility would accomplish is broadcast a message to society in general that unless it is your sperm or egg, go sit in the corner and shut the fuck up. Put your cape and collar away and stop reciting the fiction that it is society's responsibility to protect that life. If society has a responsibility to protect life, it wouldn't fail so miserably when that life is born. Just look around and tell me about the banged-up job society is doing with the lives of the born.

If you are advancing a religious agenda, realize this truth; God will decide things that God decides and your good intentions have no tangible merit in the discussion. Once the parish leaves the pews, they must use their God given free will in their lives.

And before you get your markers, poster boards and pink hats out for the pro-choice march you think I'm intending to join - let me put my purple hat on and upset you too. (Trigger warning) If the parents-to-be intend to care for the child once born, both of those parents-to-be should have near equal rights in the decision about that life. I say "near equal" because in fairness, a mother carries the child procreated by the couple and should be the driving force of the decision-making process while that child is within her.

Why not let the natural order of the universe guide the extent to which a mother and father-to-be should decide? Look at it like this, compare the size of the egg to the sperm and that proportion should be the weight of the decision-making input between the mother and father.

Before anyone asks the dumb question: "Well, then shouldn't a rapist or an abuser be given rights?"

No. Just no. My view point assumes two consenting adults to the act of procreation. Neither a rapist, nor an abuser fall into this category. Likewise, where the mother's life is in danger, it is her right of self-determination that is paramount.

What I'm talking about is the elective decision to end a pregnancy; whether or not there is a heartbeat. At a certain point in the pregnancy where the life is viable, I would add, **the decision of the child should control.**

That wasn't a moment of insanity or a typo. I mean it. If the child has progressed in their journey to the point that medical science has determined it is viable and able to otherwise survive outside the womb, there should be a presumption that the child wants to live. At that point, I think parents should have made their decisions already, and unless there was a compelling reason to end that life, the baby should be given the opportunity to live.

Before everyone on both sides of the debate begin to sharpen their pitchforks and ready their torches to chase me out of the debate, I don't have the ability to affect your decisions and wouldn't want to affect them either. If you are pregnant, I would gladly take my own advice; wish you and yours well and sit in the corner, shutting the fuck up.

Go ahead, be offended. You have that right.

RELATIONSHIPS AND THE POWER OF STANDING YOUR GROUND

According to my ex-boyfriend, 99% of women are ungrateful and I am one of them. Uh-oh. Looks like we might have a woman-hater on the loose. Someone call the United Nations Gender Equality hotline. I've flushed out a real-life, undercover misogynist. He's all yours.

Yep, I have been analyzed, categorized and classified ungrateful by a man I haven't seen in about twelve years. Although, considering I was up against such a warped conception stating that 99% of women are ungrateful, I never really had a chance at success.

So, what did I do to constitute such a radical characterization?

I no longer possess the desire to engage with him. That's it in a nutshell.

Twelve years have passed and still, he seeks me out despite the fact that I have since married another man and have unduly expressed my disinterest in him.

Over the years I have had to block him on social media and email, but every now and then I click that unblock button because I have this internal battle about blocking people that have meant something in my life. The act of blocking can feel hostile and contentious toward the blocked. It is not unlike balancing an invisible sword over their heads which in turn affects our own karma. But some people leave us no choice.

Sometimes, people can't let go.

During a recent "unblock" phase, it didn't take him long to figure out he was carrying an "Out of Jail" card. His name blinked with an incoming message on Messenger within a matter of days. How he manages to score this information so fast is beyond me. Some folks have way too much time on their hands.

Speaking of time, it is of the essence. We are all aware of that. There are only so many days to speak your truth to the people that matter in our lives.

He wasted no time in declaring his truths to me. He thought about me and my children all of the time. He couldn't forget me. Mistakes were made and he'd give anything to ease the discordant feelings still lingering deep inside. Twelve years and he is still trying for a past that will never come again. A filtered past that looks strikingly different through my eyes.

The past has a way of glamorizing the truth. The years roll by and it gets easier to peer through rose-tinted glasses existing to make everything seem beautiful by distorting the real facts. As a woman who has experienced domestic abuse for over a decade at the hands of her first husband, rose-tinted specs and the ability to romanticize the truth does not always work for me.

Truth: Some people show up in our lives to reinforce what we don't want.

I am not suggesting these people are any less important than the ones that stick around. They are just as significant because it through these interactions and relationships that we are pushed to assert ourselves; to believe in ourselves enough to stand our ground.

Life presents us with options; forks in the road that lead to alternative destinations and different realities. Thirteen years ago, and divorced, the option for me looked something this:

Would you like another serve of asshole, Kim? Or would you prefer to experience real love and respect now?

Naturally, I was opting for the latter. But, before I got to the love and respect part, I had to sit down to one more turbulent meal of asshole. In the form of Mister 99% guy. I found myself on repeat. Almost.

He waltzed into my home and wanted control from the get-go. The earliest sign was when I cooked for him for the first time, presenting a meal that was instantly met with a grimace and a rude remark. My heart dropped. His mother didn't cook that way. Turned out, his mother did everything better than me. Do I look like your fucking mother?

I should hope not. Especially when wearing black lacy lingerie, strappy stilettos and clutching a bottle of edible body oil. Vanilla flavoured. There are benefits to divorce. You get every other weekend kid-free to swing from the proverbial chandeliers. We swung hard. His mother stayed out of it.

Thank goodness.

My friends became his enemies. Not really. But if I dared smiled when greeting one of my friends, I was accused of deception.

"You haven't smiled that wide all day!"

"Umm... what the actual fuck?"

Can you image how he coped with my male friends? He loathed every one of them and didn't bother to conceal the fact.

My children became his enemies. Not really. But exerting dominance over children has a way of making narcissists feel empowered. He actually kicked my three-year-old daughter because it bothered him that she wanted to cuddle up with me on the lounge.

Red flag blazing.

I became his enemy. Not really. But I stood up for myself and my children with a fire I could not deny. A fire kindled from years of living on my nerves with an abusive husband and a promise I had made to myself - No longer would I accept ill-treatment from a man.

With each and every one of his attempts to coerce me into submission, I responded with a strength I never knew I had. Even when he physically hurt me in the most spiteful ways.

His pain was inflicted with malicious intent. Whereas, my ex-husband was an outright hothead. This guy did stuff to offend my delicate parts; like pinching my nipples till they bruised or tearing my anus so that I bled for a week. He would strike when I'd least expect it – during a hug or a play-rumble.

Yeah.

Truth: Some people show up in our lives to remind us of who we don't want to be.

Playing the victim gets old. So does the stress that comes from continually being on guard. Sometimes, people put us in a position where we have no choice but to stand by our convictions regardless of the outcome. Even if it makes us feel horrible on the inside. These are the moments that shape our lives. The forks in the road where we face a choice to either change it up or continue choosing similar experiences.

We always have a choice. Always.

Life whispered:

Are you done with mistreatment, Kim? Would you like to raise the bar and attract better experiences into your life? Are you ready for love; real love?

Yes please.

He was the catalyst in choosing to break the cycle. The final straw at the end of a long and dark road littered with abuse. Thankfully, the experience was fleeting in the grand scheme of things, lasting about six months. Although, the relationship was profound nonetheless – just in a different context to how he views it through those distorted glasses.

It was through that relationship, I learned that how we choose for ourselves is largely based on self-perception – the manner in which we view our own worth; what we're prepared to settle for and what we will fight for. I fought for respect.

I chose to be alone rather than face another long-term bout of pain and dysfunction. I chose myself and I chose my children. If that makes me ungrateful, then so be it because I'd choose it again in a heartbeat.

Sometimes, it makes sense to remove the rose-tinted glasses and see the past for what it is. If we can't do that, the lessons go unlearned and we might find ourselves on repeat while faintly hearing life whisper truths through our soul. Something like respect. Something like real love.

"The intuitive mind is a sacred gift and the rational mind is a faithful servant. We have created society that honors the servant and has forgotten the gift."
 – Albert Einstein

THE WHISPER

"Intuition is the whisper of the soul."
– J. Krishnamurti

I've heard it many times throughout my life; that inner voice whispering through my soul and guiding me forth as I've stumbled along my life path. Every day we're faced with choices; sometimes, the decisions we need to make are crucial to the way our paths unfold.

Other times, the choices are much simpler. All of the time, though, there is an unseen part of you and me that has no motive other than to love and guide us through our physical experience here on the earth plane, and that presence ultimately wants the best for us and our soul growth – the higher self.

Hold on a second, I know what you're thinking – but before you go jumping to conclusions, I'm not planning to conduct a lesson in spirituality here. That's not my gig. I'm no Wayne Dyer or Matt Kahn, although I have enjoyed their teachings. I'm no self-proclaimed guru, or Zen master either. That's not me. My intention is to create a place I can share my thoughts and perspectives. Some I've gathered through my experiences in the external world, and some I've learned from the eternal space we find within ourselves – the great silence. Besides, it's my belief that spirituality is very personal and something that needs to be experienced in order to understand.

Now, where was I?

Oh yeah, the higher self of yourself. The beautiful presence that stalks you like a shadow you just can't shake. That all-knowing, all-encompassing part of you that connects you to all things, including source energy. Actually, it's the essence of source energy, and if you understand that notion, then you'll understand what Neville Goddard and U.S. Andersen meant when they wrote "You are god." Or indeed, how powerful and symbolic the words "I am" are.

It doesn't matter whether you acknowledge this pure part of yourself as it's there regardless. How you choose to use that higher guidance is entirely your decision. Have I always listened to my inner self? No. The truth is, it has taken me many years to learn how to cultivate and nurture a relationship with this invisible part of myself and to arrive at a point where I am comfortable enough to trust it.

Can you imagine how many more years it has taken for me to gather enough nerve to even write about this stuff?

Lots and lots.

I can think of many instances when I've listened to that inner voice, even before I was self-aware enough to really grasp the reality of those rich inner layers. Of course, there's been plenty of occasions when I've chosen to ignore my inner guidance system too.

I'm going to touch on one of the times when I actually listened before I had gained enough insight and awareness about myself; the section of my life when I lived beneath the veil of ignorance. I was about eighteen years old and in the middle of a turbulent relationship (young love – you got to love it). It was a late Saturday night and my boyfriend had thrown me from the comfort of his ride and left me alone on a dark Sydney suburban street. It was punishment for standing up for myself. This guy was sweet at times but he could be a real hot-head.

I had two choices. I could walk the half-hour it would take to get home, which meant negotiating the Rockdale station overpass, or, I could go to the house nearby of my friend's boyfriend, who I'll call Grant, and ask for a ride home. Since a young woman meandering around Rockdale station alone at night wasn't considered safe, I went with the latter option. I was no dummy, no way was I going to risk a late-night stroll over that station on my own. That was rape-bait behaviour, so it was a no-brainer. Besides, I knew my girlfriend was with him that night and she would look out for me.

The decision was made, and I set off towards the house. Now, before I get to the part where I arrived at Grant's place, I need to back up a little and explain that Grant happened to have a little room at the back of his home and separate from the main house. Grant had recently allowed one of his old mates to occupy the room, which I'd frequented often with my group of friends. His mate, who was much older than the rest of us, had recently been released from a jail stint and had now taken up residence in our hang-out room.

I had met Grant's friend numerous times while always in the company of my boyfriend and friends. He seemed okay, but in all honesty, he wasn't someone I'd felt entirely comfortable around. That fact wasn't all that foreign to me, though, because seldom did I feel comfortable around people I didn't know.

Grant shared the main house with his ageing grandfather. Whenever our tribe would hang out at Grant's place, it was this back room that we'd pile into and sit around and listen to music or watch movies. A rather serious looking Pitbull terrier lived there too, and I remember being a little concerned about entering the backyard alone with this dog on guard.

The point is that I had never been in the main house, and I wouldn't dare dream of imposing on Grant's grandfather, especially at that time of the night. Therefore, it had to be the back room. However, when I'd arrived at Grant's house, I noticed his car wasn't parked in the usual spot outside on the street. Hmm. What to do? I didn't really think too hard about it at the time; it was late, cold, and I was tired. So, I decided to see if Grant's friend was still up. He had a car, and he was nice enough. He might even drive me home, or in the very least, I'd have somewhere warm to wait for Grant and my friend to get back home, right?

Right.

So, there I was, in the dark, creaking open the side gate that would lead along the narrow path towards the back room. The Pitbull turned out to be okay with my intrusion. She knew who I was and allowed me access to the premises without a fuss. She trotted alongside me as I snaked along the path and emerged into the backyard where I was confronted by the shadowy walls of the blackened back room and the sound of light snoring.

I did what any eighteen-year-old would do in my situation; I acted without thinking. I began to knock on the window of the back room and softly call the guy's name. It was very possible I'd considered this man was a member of my tribe, considering he seemed to always be around us of late. I'm pretty sure that was the driving thought. I trusted my friends, and Grant vouched for this guy. So, why start distrusting now?

A rustle sounded from the other side of the window; a slight movement accompanied by a mumble broke through the snoring, and it was at that precise moment that I froze on the spot while an overwhelming tingle zapped up my spine and whirled through my mind. My inner self was screaming at me to stop what I was doing. The message was unmistakable – keep knocking and I would find myself in a world of trouble. A clear warning to retreat.

For some reason, I didn't second guess myself that night. I listened.

My heart pounded as I quietly retraced my steps, bid the dog farewell and crossed over the creaking gate threshold. I emerged back onto the street where I sat on the brick fence outside Grant's home and waited for him and my girlfriend to arrive. Thankfully, I didn't have to wait too long in the cold, and I eventually got my ride home safely.

It would be a long time before I pondered the feelings that hit me that night. At the time, the moment passed and I got where I needed to be, and I didn't take the time to acknowledge the significant message my intuition provided. Yet, there was no mistaking that inner voice warning me to stop knocking on that window. It was strong and precise, and it gripped my senses with a loud alarm that I couldn't ignore.

I can't predict what might've happened had I awoken that man, and I shudder to contemplate how it could have played out for me. Somehow, I know that something much higher than myself was looking out for me that night – a guiding presence that sought to protect me, and I chose to listen; and for that, I give my eternal gratitude. How blessed are we to have access to the wonderous tools of intuitive guidance? If only more of us would tune into the beautiful sanctuary within us and take our cues from that divine source, I'm certain this world could reach astonishing heights in evolution. There I go doing the dreamer thing again.

I love you, John Lennon ;)

WHERE'S THE EXCITEMENT AT?

*E*veryone else had it nailed. They seemed to be sure of who they were and what they wanted out of life. My friends graduated from school with plans. I graduated with a half-baked idea of umm ... hairdressing. I think. That was after notions of becoming a marine biologist or a photographer idled through my mind.

A few years out of school I ran into a friend at a train station. I was heading home after spending the day in Sydney working a modeling shoot. It was during one of her interludes between our homeland and the States. She'd met an American fella when he was visiting Australia some years before. It was an encounter that solidified her path and had her spending much of her time in America until they eventually married and she settled there permanently.

"*How's your sex life?*"

No, she didn't say that, but it was the first thing that popped into my head when I spotted her; along with fuzzy memories of a Diesel concert, *Love Cats* and *Working Class Man*. Ah, the impression people leave in our minds – crowded school halls, The Cure and Jimmy Barnes scrawled over her canvas bag, and her staple line reserved for me when our paths collided.

"Hi Kimmm, how's your sex life?"

"Steamier than 9 1/2 Weeks."

Grin.

We both knew the only thing happening between my sheets was a whole lot of sleep after some imaginative fantasies starring Michael Hutchence, but that's what made this quirky exchange even more interesting.

I wish I could say the same when faced with her incoming statement on the station that afternoon. Sometimes, snippets of conversations can stay with you for eternity. This was one of them.

"I always thought it would be you with the exciting life and not me."

"Huh?"

I mean, what the actual fuck? I was 19 years old for crying out loud. Did she expect me to have an exciting life already? What constituted an exciting life anyway? I was smothered in studio make-up after a day beneath heavy lights and a fast stint on location, and that didn't spike her "excitement" radar? Was America where the excitement was at?

I walked away feeling somewhat flat. I didn't have an American boyfriend. My guy's idea of adventure started and began with the car engine he kept mounted in his bedroom. Throw in a Van Damme flick, a bowl of weed and some munchies and it was happy days.

I never had it sorted. The modeling career was short-lived. I discovered very fast how much I loathed being photographed, and I couldn't work out which was worse – the catwalk or the cameras. When my agent told me to drop five more kilos for a gig in Japan, I walked. I turned down an opportunity to experience excitement. Was Japan where the excitement was at?

I'll never know.

Not long after, I was walking home from the bus stop when a man drove by. He hit the brakes, chucked a "uey" and parked up ahead of me. He got out of the car with a huge grin. I was thinking I had a nutcase on my tail. Nothing new there but there was no place to go other than forward – he was on my street. I could almost spot my house if I squinted hard enough.

"*Hi beautiful.*"

"*Hey.*" Keep walking.

"*Wait – I saw you and I had to stop because I know you're perfect for a job.*"

Stop walking. I was in-between jobs and needed cash.

"What job?"

"It pays well, 100 bucks an hour plus tips. You'll get A LOT of tips, trust me."

"A-huh, what's the job?"

No, I'm not going to tell you he was looking for a hooker. He ran a high-end underground gambling house and wanted me to be their waitress-cum-eye-candy-cum-grope girl. The look on his face said it all.

He pushed a card in my hands. "*Call me. You can start right away.*"

Was working in an illegal gambling house where the excitement was at? I never made that call. I'll never know.

There was another conversation that stuck with me. When I turned 40, a friend told me that I was going to love the 40's. I was skeptical.

"*Okay, why?*"

He laughed.

"*Because those are the years you discover who you really are and begin to own it. You just don't care about as much – only the stuff and the people that matters.*"

Sounded good. Maybe even a little exciting. I wasn't sure that I believed him, though, because this was coming from a man who'd never had kids. He lived the life of a carefree artist without responsibilities. Enter wife and kids and that's all changed now. I wonder how that's working out for him. In his 40's.

. . .

But it begged the questions: **Who was I really and how would I find out?**

I was never like everyone else. I'd spent my life trying to be like everyone else and feeling at odds with myself because I wasn't. I mean, time and time again I'd turned down excitement, mostly because my idea of excitement didn't gel with the usual. Or maybe because I never knew who I really was or what I wanted.

There were years when I devoted my life to my children. They filled the void. That happens, you know. To mothers. Children can provide that sense of purpose. Except, it's a farce that cannot be sustained because we are not here for our children and nor are they here for us. They are here to fulfill their own destinies as we are.

Some people know right off the bat what they want out of life, but I never did, and I'd spent years trying to figure it out. I remember thinking that I probably didn't have a "purpose" like other people. I was just here and that had to be enough. But it never was, and it wasn't excitement that I craved; it was purpose. Soul purpose.

The moment I let go and stopped worrying about "why I was here" was the moment I knew where the excitement was at. It wasn't in America or Japan, or an underground gambling house. It was in the little things and the big things, the simple stuff and the complexities. And it was ingrained in my experiences.

Excitement is:

- Desire and yearning – feeling the pain and learning how it shapes you.
- It's in creation – carving out your life and choosing something different.
- It's taking chances, believing in yourself that little bit more and cultivating faith.
- It's listening to your gut, following your heart and claiming your joy.
- It's getting vulnerable, making mistakes and breaking the rules.
- It's passion – deep kisses that last forever and making love till the sun comes up.
- It's not caring if you lose sleep.
- It's letting the small stuff slide.
- It's feeling your baby kick for the very first time.
- It's forgiving people and forgiving yourself.
- It's taking a deep breath and telling someone you love them.
- It's pushing yourself out of your comfort zone.
- It's choosing not to play it safe.

- It's daring to dream and appreciating each step it takes to realize your dreams.
- It's failure and disappointment, then gritting your teeth and trying again.
- It's tears and missing somebody until your heart cracks.
- It's finding a message from someone special.
- It's recognizing the rare.
- It's the person that makes you feel things that you never thought possible.
- It's the one that takes your breath away.
- It's in the grit and the profane, the utterly crude and rude.
- It's the beauty and the mysterious.
- It's the sun emerging from the sea and the star soaring across the night sky.
- It's the way your heart flutters when love comes calling.
- It's learning to love yourself.
- It's in the perverted underground clubs.
- It's the hookers and hustlers working the strip.
- It's the filthy homeless man asking for a dime.
- It's getting stuck out in a summer storm and laughing like a mad person in the rain.
- It's finally being to true yourself and having the courage to follow through.
- It's plugging in and plugging out.

- It's not equating death with the end.
- It's discovering your connection to life.
- It's music and dancing like a crazy person.
- It's exploring the unknown.
- It's not being afraid to love through the storm because you know it's worth it.
- It's not being afraid to be different.
- It's the way someone looks at you.
- It's the way you look at yourself.
- It's spending time with the people you care about.
- It's finding your wings – realizing who you really are and filling in the missing pieces.
- And it's finally knowing your soul purpose and being good with however things turn out.

Excitement never eluded me; it was already there, every step of the way. And my purpose? When I stopped overthinking it and searching outside of myself for the answers it found me and I realized that too was always there. I just wasn't looking in the right places. Maybe my friend was right about the 40's after all, because these years belong to me, and I'm owning them.

SOUL SIGNATURES

THE TWIN FLAME SOUL CONNECTION SERIES BY XAVIER EASTENBRICK

SOUL SIGNATURES – PART ONE

Mirrored souls.

Is it possible that each of us share an identical energetic frequency with another soul? And that that soul can simultaneously be incarnated on earth at the same time as you? Does there exist a love so deep and so rare that everything you thought you knew about love suddenly implodes inside you like a silent percussion and pales in comparison to the connection you sense toward your mirrored soul? Your twin soul?

There is so much we do not understand about our existence here on earth and beyond, and so much more that we tend to dismiss far too easily. Why are we here? For what purpose do we arrive in a cocoon of flesh and blood and walk the earth?

Perhaps we are here to get an education, pay our taxes, wash our cars, and save our money for a rainy day. Find a good partner, get married, churn out a kid or two, maybe three. Play "happy family" and do the right thing until you retire on the edge of your dream and live out your days till you die.

And why not? It doesn't sound half bad. I guess. It also sounds ordinary, but if that is what floats your boat then who am I to question your source of buoyancy?

What if there is more, though? What if there is a part of your soul-fabric here on earth and breathing amongst the living at the same time as you? And what are the chances you would encounter this precious soul during your lifetime?

Is it such a far stretch to ponder the extraordinary when life is laced with mysterious phenomena and unforgettable magical moments? Does the idea fall so far out of your comfort zone that you would rather push away the unknown? And are your precious inner-boundaries so rigid that you cannot shatter their invisible walls to accept that which you do not understand?

Sometimes, life will present us with an exquisitely rare connection cloaked in a cryptic puzzle designed to push back against those boundaries you so long to keep erected. Messy, elegant and confronting moments that will inevitably lead to the choice between burying your head in the sand or embracing the uncharted and going with the flow of the current.

Like many of us, I have been on a unique journey since

the moment I was born. A soul-searching voyage that has taken me through rough, stormy waters to the crystal-clear lagoons of clarity I have periodically discovered along the way. I don't have the answers. My quest in seeking the truth is insatiable and endless, and with each revelation I discover, I find myself confronted with more questions. One thing that I do realize is that every moment leading to this day has been a series of fated interventions and marvellous signs that have been orchestrated in divine order for my own personal-growth experiences and revelations.

When you ask for answers, they are always given. Always.

My interest in souls and soul connections began in earnest back in 2007 after I had walked out on a dysfunctional marriage. Since then, I have navigated the days of my life utterly aware of an intelligent, all-encompassing presence that governs the universe and all that exists. That thirst for knowledge and looking beyond my physical senses has brought into my life beautiful revelations and unforgettable connections, and has led to the moment that my path collided with Xavier Eastenbrick; a special kind of man who finds himself on a sacred soul journey like no other – the Twin Flame journey.

I had the pleasure of getting together with Xavier to work with him to bring you a three-part series of blog articles that might surprise or even rattle your sceptical mind, but hopefully also broaden the scope of your thoughts to ponder the extraordinary phenomena that takes place in our beautiful world. Mostly though, it is our intention to bring clarity and offer guidance to those on the PATH and seeking answers. This blog post series is dedicated to all the Twin Flames out there. These words are for love.

> *"Love makes the impossible, possible."* – Xavier Eastenbrick.

Hello Xavier! It is such a pleasure to have you here on Undercurrent to talk about your Twin Flame experience. Can you tell us about Twin Flames, what that sacred connection means to you, and why you think there are so many misconceptions surrounding the Twin Flame phenomena?

Xavier:

"Twin Flames" is a term that attempts to crystallize in words, a phenomenon that predates the term. It is a connection that exists between two, (and only two) people who are energetically connected in soul. They are in fact, mirrors of each other and reflect the divine feminine and masculine energies which exist in each other. Those energies exist in us all, but in Twin Flames they are complementary to one another. That is not to mean they are always the same or always opposite in terms of their personalities or other identifiers of who we are, but merely complementary to each other. It is a soul connection of the highest order and is a matter of identical energetic frequency.

The reasons the discussions around Twin Flames are prone to misconceptions, as well as the unfortunate tendency of those with predatory interests to take advantage of those experiencing a Twin Flame connection, are due to the lack of awareness, misunderstandings and the general mystique surrounding the connection. You see, many of the great stories we can remember – both real and fictional, are actually Twin Flame stories. Only they were never characterized as such. The fairy tales of "happily ever after" and "always finding each other" are wonderful aspects of the journey. Yet, if people knew the hard truth of it all, they would most probably not want to aspire to engage in the Divine connection.

What people don't realize is this; you don't become a Twin Flame, rather, you simply are one. Just as you cannot close your eyes as a white person and wish yourself to become one of color, you cannot simply will yourself to be a Twin Flame. If you realized the nature of the journey and the challenges it represents, it is more than likely that you wouldn't go within 1,111 miles of being a Twin Flame, because it is hard. It's damn hard to be a Twin Flame; especially in this already complicated world.

However difficult the path, if you are a Twin Flame it is important to remember it is worth every obstacle and every ounce of pain because regardless of how corny it might seem to express this fact, it is a journey paved with uplifting moments stretched along a sacred foundation.

Sacred: it is a word we usually use in religious contexts or matters of godly connotations. If you understand the meaning of the word in the highest sense, there is a humility to it. When something is sacred, it does not seek your approval, nor does it aspire to an achievement of status. It exists in service of good; it exists in the energy and frequency of love. That is the highest and purest mission of Twin Flames – and by love, I'm not talking about some pedestrian economy of emotional exchange, I'm talking about unconditional love.

Unconditional love is loving to love without expectation of anything in return. It is loving without attachment. That is the love Twin Flames share with each other and expand in their connection. It is the love that emanates from their union and expands the universe.

Wait, what?

"Expands the universe? Xavier, have you done lost your mind, man? Surely you don't mean that literally, do you?"

Yes. Yes, I do.

Still think I'm crazy?

Ask yourself this not so simple question – What is the purpose of the universe? Is it to expand the blackness of space and turn great spheres of rock into planets and greater spheres of energy into stars? Really? That's it? Seems kind of pointless doesn't it? Science will tell you many theories about what and why things happen in the universe and perhaps even show you evidence and empirical data to support it. That is, until they have a new definition, theory and/or study that completely reverses course (Looking at you, Pluto).

Here is my perspective: The purpose, point and propagation of the universe is love. Love, in the highest sense is the self-sustaining perpetual motion energy of the source of creation in the universe. If it makes it easier to understand, love is God and God is love. I am not necessarily talking about God in the sense of Abraham, Moses, Jesus, Muhammad, Buddha, Krishna, or any other identity espoused by religion. But that deepest sense of God in the formless existence of the eternal perfect.

Breathe.

I know I just blew up your mind, but re-read it and you will see that it is actually not as complex to understand as it initially appears. Let go of the expected patterns of reality and read with the eyes of your soul. That is the point. We walk around in the life we live satisfied living beneath invisible blinders and thinking this is all there is.

Guess what? It's not.

Suddenly, we are thrust into the light of truth and awaken to who we truly are. For some, the awakened truth is their identity as a Twin Flame.

Being a Twin Flame means you accept a reality that is difficult to comprehend, and that is because it is completely alien to what you have always been taught and accepted to be true. Think about this mind bender; you were born as an individual in the world. However, you might not fit in. You may have had an unidentifiable vacant feeling within, a feeling which you accepted as your "normal". You might even feel crazy because there is a whisper of a connection to something else; something that doesn't quite make sense. Then, you have an awakening which propels you into a spiritual reality you never knew existed.

After which, you may encounter her/him; your Twin Flame who you do not necessarily know as your "Twin Flame" because the so-named concept is not even in your knowledge data-base. You feel a connection to her/his thoughts and emotions. You begin to notice signs and synchronicities – which are simultaneous occurrences of events that are connected but lack apparent causality, i.e. seeing 11:11 repeatedly, and other symptoms of being a Twin Flame.

Other Twin Flame signs and synchronicities may include:

- Mirrored or connected experiences.
- Similar or harmonious life-paths/soul urge numbers.
- Mirrored names.
- Profound dream appearances and messages.
- Feeling of intimacy.
- Noticing the Yin-Yang symbol.
- Meeting under strange and/or serendipitous circumstances.

The synchronicities and signs can be highly personal and draw you back to your Twin Flame. For example, I see '22', the star symbol and the vesica pisces. A friend I've met and come to know who also identifies herself as a Twin Flame sees her twin's given name everywhere.

Finally, after much confusion and existential crisis, you encounter information about Twin Flames and exhale in relief (and also some worry) because you now begin to understand what and who you really are;

You are a Twin Flame.

The irony about the misconceptions surrounding Twin Flames is that much of the problem is of our own doing. Let me explain. In the course of my voracious Twin Flame search for information, I have read the good, the bad and the weird, to the downright bizarre variety of information available out there. It is the bad [misinformed] and the weird that creates the impression of incredulity. In an effort to explain the happenings of Twin Flames, some tend to gravitate to typically unrelatable terms and concepts.

For example, Twin Flames experience telepathy and are connected at the energetic level. Some tend to short hand it by speaking only in terms of divinity and spiritual concepts. Which is perfectly fine, if it resonates with you, but if you aren't familiar with those concepts, they are not relatable.

Instead, if you understood the Twin Flame connection as the spiritual equivalent of quantum entanglement (Yes, I'm aware that not everyone can relate to quantum physics), it is at least relatable to something we may accept as part of our concrete reality. For those of you who may not be familiar with the phenomena of quantum entanglement, it is a phenomenon recognized by science where two particles are separated by time and space; what affects one, affects the other at the same time regardless of the distance between them. The particles are connected (entangled) and share an energetic signature.

Fine, let's say you are not ready to dive head deep into quantum physics. Think of Aspen trees. On one hand they are separate trees, but on the other hand they share the same root structure in clusters. We see many trees but they are one organism. It is not so hard to understand the interconnected separateness of trees. So, why then should it be so hard to accept the interconnectedness between two people? You might not see the connected tree roots from the ground you stand on, but that does not mean that they aren't there. Similarly, you might not see the roots between Twin Flames as they stand on the ground of your accepted reality, but it doesn't mean that they are not there.

If you can accept that concept, then accepting the reality of Twin Flames is not entirely difficult to understand.

RUNNER & CHASERS

SOUL SIGNATURES - PART TWO

"Love makes the impossible, possible."
– Xavier Eastenbrick.

The notion of one soul dividing to incarnate the earth simultaneously first came to my attention back in 2007 when reading Michael Newton's, Destiny of Souls. I remember the idea seemed so far out of my range of perception at the time that I almost immediately dismissed it as an improbability. Yet, as my life has unfolded the opposite it now true.

I have come to believe the Twin Flame journey to be an extremely personal and spiritual path – one that can only be completely understood by those experiencing it. I was so fascinated by the idea of this divine connection, that I chose to explore and write about it in my novella, Wildflower – a story included in my latest collaborative release, Untamed Destinies. It was during my research for that particular project that I discovered Xavier Eastenbrick.

For me, soul connections are a super interesting topic to ponder. I'm thinking it must be an honor and a privilege to have encountered your Twin Flame during this lifetime, but you [Xavier] mentioned that the path is not necessarily an easy one. Can you tell us more about that? Why is it that those experiencing the true Twin Flame connection suffer? And perhaps you can explain the notion surrounding what is termed as the "runner/chaser" dynamics between Twin Flames.

Xavier:

I never really had a problem with the soul splitting aspect of Twin Flames incarnating on earth because as odd as it might seem, I always felt there was a certain aspect of myself that wasn't part of me – as if I wasn't truly whole. I felt the split before I knew about it. It was just a sense, but it was a sense that was core to the development of who I am. I thought it was normal. When I encountered my Twin Flame and then discovered information about Twin Flames, those feelings I had always felt began to make much more sense.

It's funny. We accept biological twins in our society, but we find it difficult to grasp the concept of a soul splitting in much the same way. In the Sufi religion, they speak of Twin Flames as twin rings interconnected in a vesica pisces shape. This [symbolism] has always resonated with me. Of course, the question that many ask (almost hopefully) is: "Okay, the soul can split into Twin Flames. What about three or more parts?"

No. Just no.

It is complicated enough for soul-counterparts to live their lives across time and space and then find each other and deal with the connection. It would be a cruelty of cosmic proportions to split the soul into three or more parts and then have a tripartite connection. I am happy to be proven wrong, but as far as I am concerned, I reluctantly accepted Twin Flames as a reality and cannot fathom a further split of the soul.

I say "reluctantly" because my faith began from a place of scepticism and wilful doubt – I did not want to believe in any of this. I tried my damnedest to justify as much as I could, but there were core elements to the connection that were simply beyond random happenings that could be dismissed as coincidence or imagination. It is much like when one may doubt the existence of a higher intelligent design and order to the universe; whether it be named God or source energy, it is the momentum and divine will of the universe. You can try to supply a rational explanation – and then you encounter sacred geometry; the golden ratio; the universality of numbers and the Fibonacci sequencing.

Regardless of your view on religion, none of these phenomena are random. There is order to the universe and that order represents an intelligent design.

There are schools of thought within the Twin Flame community who theorize about Twin Flames being the split of the primary soul, and then there are twin rays and so on. I am not necessarily on board with those extensions because it seems to unnecessarily complicate an already complicated connection.

After many hours of research and devouring endless words surrounding the realm of soul connections, and according to my own intuition based upon my experiences thus far, I have drawn the following conclusions I believe to be true of soul connections:

- **Karmic connections** – lessons to be learned.
- **Soulmate connections** – include aspects of one's soul family – connections that resonate in a harmonious frequency and which further the soul's growth.
- **Twin Flames** – the crown jewel of soul connections – the mirror self; the counterpart of the soul; the great tempest of change. Twin Flames are the fire crucible of the soul, as well as the trigger of soul healing and betterment.

I think you get my drift. Your Twin Flame is many things and will at some point during a lifetime eventuate into a harmonious union. But much like a duet of out-of-tune instruments, in the lead up to harmony there often exists a dissonance between the souls which can be quite frustrating.

The Twin Flame journey and the life-path of a Twin Flame is complicated, very much personal and can be difficult. It should be made clear that the difficulties and pain some encounter on this journey have nothing to do with being a Twin Flame and everything to do with healing and releasing attachments and expectations instilled in our egos.

To become the best version of yourself, you need to have an extraordinary sense of self; who you are – your strengths; weaknesses; fears; insecurities; vulnerabilities; wounding; unhealed scars; the deepest and darkest aspects of one's self. It is the kind of stuff buried beneath the core of your soul that when confronted, can drive you to the brink of madness. Facing these feelings can often be turbulent, but it is in acceptance and forgiveness of ourselves that we are able to recognize our self-worth. Those are easy enough words to write, but it is a very different story when learning to acknowledge and address the process in one's soul work.

When you encounter your Twin Flame, the meeting triggers aspects of your soul to accelerate change from within. No one changes you. Anyone who tells you that change comes from without is selling you on a narrative of lies. Change can only come from within – and only when you have an understanding of the issues that require transformation and have a genuine desire to change them. This is why the Twin Flame path can be painful; because in most instances we naturally resist acknowledging our deepest truths and want to defy the idea of revolutionizing all that which with we have grown comfortable. It is amazing what we get comfortable with.

We build up defences and shut down the breadth of our hearts because the way love works in this world and among people is often unsatisfying and conditional. In reality those invisible walls are not defences but prison confines that keep out that which we fear, yet those same defence mechanisms also imprison that which should be freed. That part of my journey hasn't been painful because if I get hurt, I might erect the equivalent of velvet curtains with ropes, just like the ones you might find at a movie theatre. But eventually, I lower the ropes because I know that is not how I want to love. To me, true love means risking everything and running full force into the horizon and not away from it. It means I love like a tsunami and have the capacity to receive and accept the same kind of storm.

For example, my fear is abandonment. You know what terrifies me? Winnie the Pooh. Go ahead and laugh. But at the end of Winnie the Pooh, after we have learned to love Pooh, Piglet, Tigger and even Eeyore, Christopher Robin grows up and leaves. "If there ever comes a day when we can't be together, keep me in your heart, I'll stay there forever." That breaks my heart. Of course, there is hope: "But, of course, it isn't really good-bye because the Forest will always be there...and anybody who is friendly with bears can find it."

While the Forest may be there and anyone can find it, the thought that rattles around my head is whether anyone would want to find me there. Will my Twin Flame want to find me or will I be that teddy bear languishing at the bottom of some closet until someone donates me to good will?

It sounds silly, but every time I see Toy Story 2, I cry at that one scene when Jessie recalls how she was once loved by her Emily and then, Emily grew up and Jesse was eventually forgotten and finally put into a box and donated to good will. She was abandoned. That is the way I have felt most of my life.

I'm Pooh. I'm Jesse.

I had to face abandonment in order to transcend beyond that fear. Two divorces and deaths of those closest to me – all of these experiences reinforced the fears while giving me the tools to deal with it. Separation from my twin also crushed me on the inside and triggered an awful dark night of the soul. An experience that was so dark, I almost couldn't distinguish between the shadows from the night. But no matter how dark I plunged, or how far I fell into the depths of fear, my soul was resilient and I survived. I found the tools within to mitigate fear and pull myself out of the darkness. I stand on my own and the one person who I can always rely on to stay with me is me. And that is the point. Many will focus on union with their twin as opposed to becoming the best, strongest version of themselves.

Those on their Twin Flame journey do not have to suffer, or at least don't have to endure prolonged suffering. It is all a matter of perspective and choosing to surrender your will and expectations. What I mean is that while we participate in fate, we do not control nor can we accelerate divine timing. It happens when it is supposed to happen and no sooner. The sooner we accept this, the sooner we can heal.

Think of it like this: a mother and a child are in the kitchen. The mother says to the child, "do not go near the stove, it will burn you." The child goes near the stove, touches the lit burner and gets burned. The mother soothes it and reminds the child not to go near the stove. At this point, if the child has learned his/her lesson, they will not get burned again. If the child goes ahead and touches the stove again, they will endure more pain. It is not much different here. The lessons are roughly the same.

If you feel pain in separation, ask yourself why you are

feeling pain. Is it a matter of your fear? Is it a matter of your attachment to an expectation or an expected outcome? The most difficult aspect of this journey to process is unconditional love. When it feels all warm, fuzzy and happy, it is easy to say you love someone unconditionally. It is when it all turns upside down that conditions pop up. That is when you can actually understand how challenging it is to love unconditionally.

Twin Flames often engage in a dance of push and pull – more commonly, and unfortunately referred to as the "runner and chaser" phase. The thrust of it stems from the fact that there is usually a Spiritual Twin who has awoken earlier and is in fact a guide for the other; the Matrix Twin. The Matrix Twin is living their life and has not yet awakened. They might not even know about Twin Flames or understand or acknowledge the connection. They might be freaked out about what they are feeling. And the rub of it all is that the Spiritual Twin can't just tell the Matrix Twin that they are a Twin Flame and more specifically, their Twin Flame. In short, it is a bittersweet paradox.

In matters of soulful truth, you must arrive at your own knowledge and understanding. It is not simply a matter of wanting to be something. You need to feel and experience it for yourself, and all the convincing in the world will not make it happen. The Matrix Twins have to believe and until they do, they won't.

"But why would anyone run away from someone who loves them and who they love?"

That is the logical question a Twin Flame might ask in this dynamic, but it is not as simple as it seems.

When you encounter your Twin Flame, you are encountering someone who is both an entirely familiar soul; your soul and yet, at the same time, a riddle wrapped in mystery with a bow tied in a quagmire – Who the hell are you and why do you love me? What is going on with me? Why do I love this person and why are they on my mind all the time? Oh wait, this is starting to frighten me! This is intense. Defences up. Denial; denial; denial. Then, "fight or flight" kicks in and suddenly, there is a Twin Flame sized hole in the wall and a dust trail leading away from you.

You are beside yourself with shock. So, you put on your sneakers and start chasing them, yelling: "Wait. I think you just didn't hear me. I said I love you! That's all. Come back!" Sometimes they run even faster. Sometimes they might hide in the woods. Sometimes, they might run to a familiar romantic interest. Who isn't you.

Are they doing it to hurt you?
No.
Are they trying to forget you?
They might be.
Do they love you?

As incredible as it might seem, they do love you and it scares the living daylights out of them.

I know what a nonbeliever would say – exactly what I would have said: "Oh, just let them go and move on. You're just reeling from an unrequited love and they just aren't into you. This was all a stupid crush and now it's over. You aren't connected to anyone. It's just part of life."

Here's the part where I tell you something unexpected; they are part right.

Of everything a nonbeliever might say – which is patently wrong – they would be correct in advising you to let them go. Surrender. If they are your twin, let them go and they will be back. Don't chase them; whether it be in reality or energetically. Give them space to deal with the complex panoply of emotions and the crisis management they are dealing with. Remember that this is an eternal soul connection and lifetimes are not the Endgame. Your encounter is enough and if and when they choose to return or if the divine timing of the universe conspires to bring you together again, you will have them back.

Some words of advice: don't let your ego and pride get in the way. Just because you may have realized who and what they are and are able to deal with the intensity of it all, be gentle in your understanding of their reaction. Forgive them as if they are the prodigal twin.

Remember, the love between Twin Flames is unconditional. That means you send them your love even in separation and in silence. You send them your love with no expectation that they'll ever love you back. You send them your love even if they hurt you and abandoned you; even if they chose someone else over you.

It's hard and can feel painful at first, but this is not a typical love story of boy meets girl and happily ever after in this lifetime. It might just be, but often times it takes many lifetimes of learning the dynamics of love to become the soul who can face their counterpart without fear and handle the intensity of the connection.

THE AWAKENING

SOUL SIGNATURES - PART THREE

Xavier, the way you have expressed the depth of your experience is unbelievably authentic and moving – thank you for sharing your inner-most feelings with us. I think it is those souls seeking the answers and in need of knowledge that will innately gravitate to and discover your words here, because although the Twin Flame journey is truly sacred, the connection can also be extremely confusing at times.

You have told us about the awakened or Spiritual Twin, and how it is for their benefit to focus on their own soul growth rather than attempting to chase or initiate union with their Matrix Twin. What advice, if any would you give to the Matrix Twin – the one feeling uncomfortable with the intensity and nature of the connection?

. . .

Xavier:

I appreciate being given the opportunity to address your questions in this setting. In doing so, I hope by sharing my experience it helps those reading it as much as it helps me writing it. All too often, people try to keep their spiritual selves bottled up and locked away for fear of being ridiculed or ostracized. Perhaps this is why people can feel crazy on this journey.

To put it into perspective, you may find more understanding and empathy talking about addiction than you do talking about the Twin Flame journey. No one would call someone addicted to drugs "crazy" – but as soon as you start talking about your soul being split and sharing existence with another human being for the purpose of breaking limitations and shattering the obstacles to love, and by doing so expanding the breadth of unconditional love – people tend to think you have lost your mind.

What I attempt to do through my writing, is to organize my Twin Flame experiences and relate them to circumstances others can identify with; therefore I gain a more grounded understanding that I can share with others.

Figuratively speaking, I take a bowl of spaghetti and comb it out. The path is daunting for so many reasons; not the least of which is the fact that the normal and typical Twin Flame process begins by experiences which occur without having learned the information ahead of time.

What I mean is that we learn to walk and then call it walking. Then, you realize you aren't walking but dancing, and not just dancing but waltzing. And then, that penultimate moment arrives when you realize you've been dancing with someone you didn't even know was there. If you are on the Twin Flame journey, that sentence makes perfect sense to you.

DISCOVERING I AM A TWIN FLAME, AWAKENING AND ENCOUNTERING MY TWIN FLAME:

Before I awakened or knew anything of substance about Twin Flames, I suppose I was living a normal life. I am not employed in any spiritual occupation or business. The experiences I have had led me toward a certain path and body of wisdom.

While much of the information I read about Twin Flames resonated with me, there were aspects of the journey I felt compelled to add to the discussion: I was able to provide a much-needed perspective on this often-complicated connection. That's the beauty of spirituality. You can be anyone or anything; a carpenter; a merchant; a fisherman; an attorney – or whatever, and still have something significant to add to the conversation about spirituality.

What I write about is based upon all that I have experienced, learned through my mistakes, as well as learning from others who have provided their written guidance. I combine the knowledge I have gathered along the way with these golden nuggets, my own education gained through schooling and through life, as well as a healthy respect for both religion, spirituality and science to inform what has resulted in the culmination of my knowledge surrounding Twin Flames.

Kim:

Can you explain how someone would know if they are in fact a Twin Flame incarnated simultaneously with their counterpart? Is there a magic flag that waves above your twin's head when you first encounter them?

Xavier:

Discovering my Twin Flame was part of my spiritual awakening process, which occurred a few years after I came to know her. From the moment I spoke with her, I was drawn to her. What she inspired within me was an incredible explosion of creativity and life-changing momentum. In the beginning, while I knew nothing about Twin Flames, somehow, I knew she was extraordinary and meeting her would be the line of demarcation between who I was and who I would become.

For the purpose of context, my journey began long ago and without it being identified with the term, Twin Flame. Growing up, I felt always odd, out of place and felt an unidentifiable sense of incompleteness. I suffered from depression and threw myself into creative projects as a way to channel my emotions.

In most of what I drew or wrote, there was an overarching theme of duality. It was something that persisted in everything I did. In fact, when I was a teenager, I remember a psychologist asked me: "If you were to draw a portrait of yourself, what would it look like?" My answer was: "I would have to draw two portraits."

At the time of my awakening, I was going through serious problems which I didn't want to talk about for reasons I won't explain here. The thrust of them were internalized stressors which built up and I was caught in a feedback-loop problem; perseveration, poor reaction; depression.

Repeat. The essence of it was that I was living an inauthentic life and it was catching up to me, tormenting my soul. I was able to mask my abysmal self-esteem with a pleasant smile and outward confidence. If you interacted with me, I was outwardly normal. Inside I was a wreck of self-loathing and nearing the bottom of the proverbial barrel.

I began to learn more and more about crystals because of a creative passion – which was inspired by my Twin Flame and then, I began to incorporate them into my life. I was drawn to certain crystals and felt their vibration. On the day of my awakening, which happened to be my Twin Flame's birthday, I was alone at home and meditating in an attempt to calm my mind. At this point, the stress feedback was the thought equivalent of a cacophony of out of tune instruments.

Weeks before I had read articles about music attuned to 432hz – a frequency known as Verdi's A and is mathematically consistent with the Universe. The American Federation of Musicians adopted the 440hz standard for pitch and most music uses that frequency.

I figured if I am going to connect with the universe, I may as well use its frequency. Accordingly, I placed certain crystals over specific chakras and played the 432hz music. I tried to silence the stress in my mind with positive imagery.

For some reason, the image of a large majestic oak tree with golden luminescent leaves and branches popped into my head. I was sitting beneath the tree and it felt so right to be there. I was almost at peace but somehow, I knew I wasn't supposed to be alone. That sense of incompleteness remained.

I began to imagine the closest people in my life with me under the tree. Each time nothing felt different. Then, I imagined her with me under the tree; the woman who I would later understand to be my Twin Flame and suddenly, everything changed.

Immediately, the lucid dream shifted. It was as if I [my energy] was pulled into a worm hole, deep in space. The scene was surreal yet authentic, and I can still describe the stunning stars, colors and galaxies I saw before my eyes and in the distance. In retrospect, while it seemed like only my energy, it is more accurate to say "our" energy, because I know it would not have been possible without her being a part of the imagery experience.

I felt a sense of wholeness I had not previously known. Our energy was propelled into deep space and continued to expand outwardly. I ceased to feel my body at all and lost the ability to comprehend my individual self. I felt all of my emotions evaporate and incredibly, I didn't love any particular person. An overwhelming rush of pure love for all things took hold within me. It was unconditional love; dependent upon nothing and no one, and it encompassed the entire universe. I let go and surrendered, and ultimately became fully conscious of my soul and all it connects to.

After a while, I felt the turmoil in my mind ease and suddenly, as if called back to my physical self, I felt the weight of my body and the familiar sense-of-self drift back into my awareness again. When I awoke and looked at my surroundings, everything I saw emanated with an aura for a few minutes.

As you might expect, it took me a while to unpack this surreal experience and figure it all out. Almost immediately, I began to see the synchronicities relating to twin soul incarnations – especially 11:11, as well as the rest of the number sequences. I kept feeling a gentle nudge to investigate the numbers I was seeing until I understood what they meant. I furiously read all about synchronicities and one of them mentioned the term, Twin Flames.

Number sequences specific to the Twin Flame phenomena:

Numbers can play a major role when the universe is communicating with you. All you have to do it look out and be aware of the signs. The universe will never fail to provide signs, symbols and synchronicities. Often, the synchronicities take the form of repeating numbers and there are numbers significant to the Twin Flame journey.

In my case, I observe triple repeating numbers and palindromes. I also notice 1010, 1111, 1212, 121, 222, as well as other sequences involving the outer number reflecting the inner number. As part of my Twin Flame research, I discovered that the number 11 is prevalent.

I had vaguely heard about Twin Flames in the past,

but never read too much about the concept. I thought it was just some fancy phrase for a "soulmate". However, the more I read and researched about Twin Flames, the more I was able to recall details which completely fit with who I would ultimately recognize as my twin. Each sign and synchronicity I see and feel now inevitably relates to her. And although she is unawakened, each divine trail the universe reveals to me leads back to her; and only her. When I recall our past discussions, the way we interact, then separated before finding each other again, it all fits the established Twin Flame connection. Through meditation and inner-work, I connect to her higher-self on a regular basis and I am able to sense her thoughts and emotions.

She is unaware of our connection and I will not be the one to tell her because she has to discover that knowledge on her own, if at all. That is one of the frustrating realities of this journey; there are no shortcuts and information cannot be served. It must be found and experienced.

In the beginning, it was difficult to navigate the connection and I quickly became the chaser, but I eventually understood the futility of it, so I chose to surrender.

In surrendering, I found peace in the form of knowing that divine timing will bring us together when it is right, if at all. And I'm at peace with fates ultimate hard reality; that this may not be the lifetime in which we reunite. What keeps me from delving into bouts of depression is my core belief and mantra: Love makes the impossible, possible.

MY TWIN FLAME ENCOUNTER – KNOWING:

Recognizing your Twin Flame is a matter of "knowing". It is a core sense; a strange sense which emanates from the soul. It is as if your insides were reading a book, suddenly looked up and saw your Twin Flame. It is what many call the feeling of being "home". The knowing occurs after the encounter and might not happen immediately. Once the knowing happens, the war begins between your brain and your heart.

WHAT HAPPENS:

The typical path usually occurs in this sequence: initial encounter, a sense of heightened awareness for your counterpart that leads to "knowing", and then, information which confirms the connection. The encounter can and usually does occur without knowing and the knowing isn't necessarily instant. This process can take a while to happen, but when it does happen, it is as if your soul clicks into place like a machine with giant gears releasing an immense sphere that rolls down a slide to a perfectly fitting hole.

. . .

BRAIN VS HEART:

Both the brain and heart can agree on processing the encounter with your Twin Flame, but it is the knowing part that is an extraordinarily difficult concept for the mind to reconcile. You typically do not register the person as your "Twin Flame" during the initial encounter. To your brain and heart, they may simply be another person. When the knowing finally hits you, it goes against everything rational about your identity as a single mortal life because your Twin Flame isn't just some love at first sight interest; they are much more than that. This is the person who encapsulates the same soul as yourself – they are literally your eternal soul in front of you.

Some mistake a strong love or a soul connection with a Twin Flame. This is not because they are ignorant, but because they may have learned about Twin Flames prior to encountering who they believe to be their Twin Flame. But when the connection is true and one or both counterparts arrive at "knowing", there is no mistaking it. This is why those who have some knowledge about Twin Flames generally suggest to others NOT to seek out information or attempt to learn about Twin Flames unless you are on the path.

BRAIN:

In an effort to protect you, your brain will fight you at

every turn and doubt almost everything. It is like white blood cells that begin attacking healthy tissue because the autoimmune system mistakes it for a disease. Your brain is framed by your ego and because Twin Flames are primarily spiritual, it is mostly contrary to what your ego accepts as reality.

For example, your ego has little problem accepting the concept of love or in loving another person who loves you back. It is a logical jigsaw puzzle of connectivity. But your ego has a big problem with the concept of the soul and in the case of Twin Flames; your soul also existing in another. If the problem the ego has with the soul can be likened to a fire, the concept of Twin Flames would be napalm.

In my case, I'm an over-thinker. I have never met a simple answer I could not first dissect into a chaos of more questions and with enough variables to choke the most pedantic philosopher. When I encountered my Twin Flame, my brain and heart were focused and aligned. I loved her in an instant, but it was too powerful to call love. The "knowing" was there too – but it was amorphous and without a convenient description to articulate in words. At first, as the symptoms of the connection began to manifest, I simply went with them because I had ways of explaining them.

For example; I suddenly became healthier and

overloaded with positive, kinetic energy, which was something I simply enjoyed as a lifestyle change. Consciously, I knew she was connected to it, but my ego wasn't necessarily bothered. The inspiration and explosion of creativity – also connected to her – was something I just accepted.

When the telepathy and emotional connection to her began to materialize and my full-blown spiritual awakening occurred with her at its heart, my ego became agitated. A sense of discomfort led to my brain trying to minimize what she meant to me or any connection at that level. I chalked it up to probable, temporary insanity or a side effect of the increase in energy or dietary changes. I tried anything I could to rationally explain what I was experiencing, even if it made less sense than what was actually happening. And to compound the issues, she was unaware as far as I knew.

Every morning was the same – she was my first thought. No matter what I was doing as each day progressed, she was constantly in my thoughts and emotions. Every night, the last thought I had before I drifted off to sleep was of her. I knew I loved her but I wondered whether I was becoming obsessed. An obsession is an unhealthy fixation or addiction to something. An obsession has a deleterious effect on the person.

With her in mind, it was not the all-consuming thought that obsession creates. She wasn't debilitating to my life. To the contrary, her affect was overwhelmingly positive in my life. Everything that involved her or was inspired by her, resulted in me at my personal best and even better than I had reason to be. I easily lost the concept of time and was singularly focused on each and every task, assignment or project at hand. I was on fire!

HEART:

Then, something unusual began to occur – I started to feel emotions which had no connection to me and made no sense of what was actually happening in my life; and I could find no rational reason for experiencing those feelings. I would be at my desk at work or in my basement and suddenly become giddy or burst out crying. I was bewildered because there was no underlying cause for me to feel that way. While I can't definitively say those emotions were coming from another person, I know for sure they were not my own.

Later, after communicating with my twin I discovered I was able to confirm a factual link to the emotions I was sensing in real time. The emotions were hers. If she fell in love, I felt it in my heart chakra as a sharp pain. When her heart broke, mine did also – in the form of a pain that felt like a heart attack. I could literally feel her energy; her times of peace and harmony, as well as her bouts of extraordinary confusion.

Ironically, the aspect that my ego had most difficulty processing was the fact that I was able to distinguish between my own emotions and those of my twin. At a certain point my ego had to admit the connection was real because it ran out of rational explanations. Doubts cloak of shadows could no longer eclipse the light.

WHEN KNOWING SETS IN:

When the luxury of doubt finally dissolved, I was left with acceptance and the full awareness that she is my twin. That is when the "knowing" set in. It was like a harmony of the various aspects of my being, all saying at the same time: "She is my Twin Flame. It is her. It has always been her."

THE PARADOX:

There are many paradoxes in the Twin Flame journey. One such paradox is that the usual path is begun by neither party realizing that they are a Twin Flame. The two in question will experience unexplained synchronicities, and perhaps even odd circumstances which may lead and guide one and/or both along the path, but the moment of realization is not accompanied with an "ah-ha" moment escorted with the skies opening up and a beam of divine light spelling out "TWIN FLAME" in burning violet letters.

Kim:

Oh, so there is no magic flag...

Xavier:

No, I'm afraid there is no magic flag!

Each Twin Flame path is specific to the set of Twin Flames, but there are enough commonalities that we are able to identify specific traits relating to the sacred connection.

For example; there is a Spiritual Twin – usually the predominantly divine feminine, and a Matrix Twin – usually the predominantly divine masculine. It is important to remember that Divine Feminine doesn't necessarily mean female and Divine Masculine doesn't necessarily mean male.

The Spiritual twin typically has an individual spiritual awakening first [either before or after they have encountered their twin]. During the course of their awakening, the Spiritual Twin will eventually become attuned to their Twin Flame – sensing there is something profoundly important about their counterpart – and will finally discover the knowledge about

Twin Flames. Think of it in terms of being asleep. You wake up, make some coffee, cook your eggs, pop in the toast and slice up some fruit. Afterwards, you finally learn that you have made this thing called "breakfast". The added kicker is that you have made breakfast for two and you're not sure why.

The Matrix Twin is called such because he is accustomed to the 3D world and as such, has immersed himself/herself in those customary ways of doing things. Spirituality might be a foreign concept to him and he might not even grasp the idea or be able to acknowledge the synchronicities and signs which might be occurring – even if those signs are howling in his face like a wild storm. Think Clark Kent without knowing he's Superman, figuratively speaking of course.

These roles lead to the push-pull dynamics of the Twin Flame journey and process. Because "running" and "chasing" sound rather predatory, I try to avoid it. It is simply the process of encountering fear and overcoming it, triggering and strengthening, and wounding and healing. If we look at it in this context, perhaps the pain can be better understood and both twins can learn from it.

It is always tempting to tell your twin that they are your twin. But try to think of it in terms of the natural order of the universe. Things progress as they should, and in the correct time they need to. A tree begins life as a seed which finds its way into the earth, interacts with nutrients and rain, before sprouting from its shell. After a while, the roots begin to anchor as the seedling pierces the surface and grows towards the sun. If you were to deny the seed this journey, no tree would appear. Similarly, telling your twin may be more about you shocking the process and imposing your own will and timing on the universe, as opposed to you surrendering and allowing the process to unfold naturally. When we try to force our will on the universe, it typically does not end well.

Instead of shocking the process, be there for your twin. Enjoy your twin, send them unconditional love in plenty, introduce them to spirituality if they are so inclined, and be part of their journey. Give them every tool they need to recognize the door to knowledge; the wisdom to unlock it; the strength to turn the key; the will to grasp the door knob and push on the door. When they are ready, be there when they find the courage to walk through the door because they will need you to be there as their Spiritual Twin in the same way you need them.

I'm not going to sugar coat it – here's the thing – this journey is HARD and the pain can be almost unbearable. Sometimes, you want to scream: "Wake up, my Twin!" because it is so damn frustrating. You become frantic with excitement to have found this extraordinary soul; your soul, and you look at any time spent apart as wasted time. I get that, truly I do.

In those times of pain, my advice is to meditate and reflect on the situation. Drop your attachments and shed your fear. Attempt to understand where your pain is coming from. Be gentle with your twin, even when they are testing your every nerve and last sprig of sanity. Be as gentle as if you were opening your front door to them, or setting that plate of breakfast down in front of them.

I began this journey from the ground level, a place of not knowing. I use my hunger for knowledge to acquire information and learn all I am capable of learning. Then, I take all the material offered, process and sort until I am able to make sense of it as much as I can. I try to keep grounded in all that I learn and focus my efforts on sharing with others that need the advice and guidance, to serve others experiencing their own Twin Flame journey.

That is an important aspect of the Twin Flame journey; to understand that we are not only part of a connected universe, but as Twin Flames, we are part of a connected community of souls who deserve our empathy, love and understanding. If I can help those on the path find their groove, maintain their sanity, faith and hope – help them understand and mitigate their own suffering, both in this process and in healing their past wounds, then I am fulfilling part of my mission to change the world.

As I set about helping other Twin Flames, it is my desire that we proceed down our respective paths and, in the process, understand Love in its purest, energetic signature and resonate a frequency so high, that it further expands the universe.

Do you want to know the reason why, as a Twin Flame, I help and serve others? The reason has nothing to do with money – I don't charge a dime – or fame – which I don't have – or anything else which might serve as a motive for one's efforts. The reason is love and the fulfilment of a simple truth I have learned; Love makes the impossible, possible.

THANK YOU

A special thank you to you for taking the time to read and journey through the pages of this book. I hope you found some resonance as well as some laughter throughout the pages that documented our personal stories and anecdotes about life, death, love & connection – we're all in it together.

No one escapes the human condition; the trials, tribulations and happiness that we experience as we wade through life. In sharing our personal stories, we are able to strengthen the invisible bonds connecting us, as well as help make our beautiful world a nicer place.

Please reach out whenever the urge strikes – I'm always around!

Be happy. Be loved. Be well.

With love,

Kim

Kim Petersen

Kim Petersen is a USA Today Bestselling Author, author of The Ascended Angels Chronicles, and co-author of the Stone the Crows series. Her debut novel, Millie's Angel received a gold award in the 2017 Dan Poynter's Global eBook Awards.

Kim is a regular contributor for Medium publications like, P.S. I Love You, The Ascent and Curiosity Never Killed the Writer, to name a few. Her articles are frequently curated by the Medium team.

Find Kim at Whispering Ink:
https://whisperinginkpress.com/
Twitter: https://twitter.com/kimpetersen_

Xavier Eastenbrick

Xavier Eastenbrick is a soul on a journey of life, meeting souls along the way. He adds to the richness of the universe and is grateful for each moment.

Find Xavier online at:
Quora: http://bit.ly/2svINGT
Pinterest: http://bit.ly/xaviereastenbrickpint
Twitter: https://twitter.com/eastenbrick

www.ingramcontent.com/pod-product-compliance
Lightning Source LLC
Chambersburg PA
CBHW030253010526
44107CB00053B/1696